Tony Kirkland

A Journey to The Stream

Passage to Purpose

ajourneytothestream.com

Copyright ©2014 by Tony Kirkland

All rights reserved. This book or any portion thereof may not be reproduced or used in any manner whatsoever without the express written permission of the publisher except for the use of brief quotations in a book review.

Printed in the United States of America

First Printing, 2014

ISBN 978-0-9913615-1-9

Library of Congress Control Number: 2013923544

www.ajourneytothestream.com

Dedication

*This book is dedicated to Mark Eric Martinez,
a dear friend whose death inspired this work.*

I'd like to thank the following people:

*Ridhwaan Harnaker and Magdalena Zukowski, both of whom worked
tirelessly with me for the past two years in this work.*

*Michael Sanow, who inspired me to go deeper into this journey and was a
huge supporter at a very important time.*

*Aranda Sundarlal for her superb editing and creative insights. The
other editors: Amanda Ross McDonald, Lorissa Bouwers, Vangi
Pantazis, and Gayle Roberts.*

Susan Batson, the best acting coach in the world, who launched my career.

Tim Mosh, leader of Chasing Summers, whose creative genius inspires me.

George Eadie, for making me finish this book.

Contents

About the Author i

Introduction iii

Prologue vii

1 Cathy 1

2 The Journey 13

3 Beginning at the Beginning 19

4 Either Way 25

5 Faraway 39

6 Loss 53

7 Plenty 67

8 Contentment 79

9 Mastery 91

About the Author

Tony Kirkland, MS, was a practicing psychotherapist in private practice in New York City for over 15 years. Over the course of the subsequent 15 years, he created a program called Structural Alignment™, which allows for radical transformation of seemingly intractable problems.

I grew up on the mean streets of Harlem, New York City, which gave me street smarts. Harlem had a very strong community at the time, in addition to its rougher side, and I learned from both. As much as I appreciated the lessons, I never really felt that was my place. Instead, I always saw a better life for myself, and the degree of suffering and destruction scared me enough to know I never wanted to live a life like that. I felt that no one should live a life like that, so I decided at the age of 14 I was going to become a psychotherapist. I didn't plan to be just any psychotherapist, but the best in the world: the Michael Jordan of psychotherapists.

I worked tirelessly on this goal from the age of 14, working as a CIT (Counselor in Training) for the YMCA in New York. I became a camp counselor, taught new counselors, and even briefly became assistant camp director. It was a great experience. I became a therapist and had a very successful private practice in New York City. Over the years, in working with clients, I found the classic model of psychology to be too limiting, so I became a coach. I did that for another 15 years and over time developed a whole new method, called Structural Alignment™.

Structural Alignment™ came about because I was working through my own personal struggles, and none of the things I tried was really working for me anymore. I'd become overly coached or overly counseled: I'd become a terrible patient. Self-analysis, psychotherapy, the forum, EFT, you name it—nothing worked for me. You could say that Structural Alignment™ was developed because

I needed to invent my own cure! This was the only process that was smarter than I was. I couldn't out- maneuver it; I had to surrender. This is still a journey for me because I often want to take control again. Then I'm reminded of the folly of that strategy....

Today I teach coaches in the Structural Alignment™ method at **SAcoaching.com**. If this is something you might be interested in exploring for yourself or your company, drop me a line at **Tony@SAcoaching.com**.

With this book, I invite you to take your own journey, and I'd love to hear from you about it. You can join one of our communities, or just say hi, at: ajourneytothestream.com

INTRODUCTION

This book is about a new way of thinking and how to have what we want in life. Think about how we live. Most of us hop from one goal to the next. To what end? Does chasing those goals ever really bring us lasting happiness? Don't we need to follow ever bigger and higher goals? What's the alternative? The whole world revolves around this notion of goal achievement, yet the most successful people—as measured by their goal achievements—are never guaranteed happiness. Why do we buy into this?

The answer is we don't know an alternative. We stay busy pursuing goals, so we don't have to face the things that really scare us, like not being loved or losing the things that matter to us. The secret is that it's an illusion: No matter what we love, it changes. Our kids, our bodies, our relationships—they all change. Where are we all racing to then?

Imagine this headline: *Man Dies of Starvation at Buffet because He Couldn't Decide What to Eat.*

Obviously, you would think that was some kind of joke. The truth is that—although not literally—it happens every day. There are people dying of loneliness while surrounded by a sea of people. How many people live in poverty in the US, even though it's the richest country in the world? Why do we starve when we are surrounded by what we want?

The answer is that the reason for the starvation is not external, but internal. Here's an idea. What if Starvation were a place we could visit? Who would want to go there for their summer vacation? This book explores the idea that there are places where we gather and suffer together. Then we call it *reality*. The world is divided into six communities. Each one has its own brand of suffering, from the people who have so much they don't know what to do with it; to the people who have so little they can barely survive. These collective pockets are places we can visit, or we can move in permanently. Worse, we can have different parts of our lives living in different places. Often, we see examples of very rich people who are starving for love, or people who are rich in loving families and communities but are very poor.

This book explores two worlds: one that we can see around us and another that we can't see. Imagine a virtual world that determines what we experience in the real world; it's like living in a video game. Imagine belonging to a place called Shortage and Starvation in the virtual world and having that cause Shortage and Starvation in the real world.

If that were true, it would mean that getting what we want is just a matter of changing our character's location!

That's the idea presented in this book: there really is a place of real joy, a place where things don't change arbitrarily, and we can have whatever we want, for as long as we want. That place is in our higher self. For some, it is our God self… whatever you call it, the idea is that our suffering comes from a separation from ourselves. Instead of reconnecting with our inner selves, we grasp for things like status and safety.

The premise of the book is that the world we've come to know is a manifestation of that separateness. There are six places of separation (represented by towns). Each place provides refuge from some form of fear but also leaves us stuck. The choice becomes either to confront the fear or to remain stuck. The journeys of the six people in the book are based on composites of real people. I chose each character as representative of a group of people I know who are stuck. The characters begin their journey together with varying levels of apparent success in life, but they all have one thing in common: they are stuck. There is no judgment of any of them, as they each represent a part of each of us. Everyone is stuck in some area of life, be it in relationship, finances, health, etc.

As the characters travel through a virtual journey, through the six towns, each town becomes more difficult to leave than the last, and there is no skipping any town. In order to move forward, each person must confront the thing that is most challenging for them.

This is why it is so hard for people to progress. Often, moving forward means letting go of things that hold us back, and that can be difficult, especially when we love those things. It's hard to let go of something bad but familiar in favor of the unknown. This is the dilemma the characters face. The promise of paradise often isn't sufficiently compelling to move us forward, especially when things aren't that bad where we are.

The Journey to the Stream is a book about faith. It is the faith that if you surrender to the right journey, then life will get better and better. What's required is faith that at the Stream, you will have everything you have ever wanted, and more.

There are many books that speak of life as an unreal journey. This is not one of them. Rather, this book examines the idea that there are two realities: one above ground and one below. The above-ground reality we can see, taste, and in it we experience every joy and pain. More importantly, however, the 'below-ground' reality, unseen, is what is causing everything to happen above ground. As a former therapist, 'below ground' meant the subconscious. That fails to capture the essence of this model, though; neurology would be a better model. Imagine physical places in the brain that determine whole clusters of thoughts and feelings. Now imagine that instead of that brain belonging to a single person, that there is just one brain, which we all share. In that model, we would meet each other in those same places and share those thoughts and feelings….

Approached this way, we can try to have what we want by working hard above ground, or we can travel below ground to get it instead, from the source. Ultimately, this book is not about getting or having things, although that happens naturally as a consequence; it is instead about having greater access to our high self.

Finally, I say *greater access* because we each have varying degrees of access to the higher self already. In that sense, there is always a part of us at the Stream, but there is a difference between having access to it and living completely from it.

In the end, we can't take the journey to the Stream alone, for none of us are truly alone. Surrendering is part of the journey to the Stream. We must surrender and realize that we have only one higher self, which is shared by all. The journey to the Stream is, in part, a practice of letting go—letting go of what doesn't work. It's practicing faith that life will always get better when we do.

Letting go, without support, is hard. We have a growing community of people on this journey. Come join us at: AJourneyToTheStream.com

Prologue

There was darkness all around her. She tried to move, but her arms felt stuck to her sides. She tilted her head, hoping to see light.

There wasn't any.

Get me out of here!

She tried to scream, but something filled her mouth, choking her. Dirt?

She tried to move her fingers and kick her legs, but it was impossible. Whatever was around her was resisting her movement.

She struggled desperately, but made no progress. Exhausted, she stopped trying. As she lay there, very still, fear engulfed her.

Tears began to run down her face, and her sobs grew harsher and louder. The more she gulped for air, the more dirt entered her mouth. She tried hard to contain her weeping, if only to save her breath.

What's happening to me?

She was trapped. Stuck.

She was buried alive.

CHAPTER 1

Cathy opened her eyes. She lay still for a few moments, staring at an unfamiliar blank ceiling above her. She didn't know where she was or why she was there. All she knew was that her head was pounding.

She remembered her 41st birthday. *Was that yesterday?* She'd gotten up at 6:30 am, as usual, and had breakfast with her family. A special breakfast, of course—her children made animal-shaped pancakes, and her husband served her breakfast on their fancy china, while all she'd had to do was sit back and relax. Her family had even done the dishes.

How she'd wound up in the bathroom contemplating suicide—that was something she couldn't quite work out.

Cathy thought of her children smiling at her over syrupy, misshapen pancakes. She thought of the colorful noodle necklace they made for her birthday. Her husband Arthur had promised her a romantic weekend getaway to any destination of her choice. It had been perfect.

The truth was that her whole life was perfect. She had a loving husband, beautiful children, her dream home, and enough money for all of them to live comfortably. Even so, something just didn't feel right. She just didn't feel perfect inside.

Cathy looked down and realized she was wearing a hospital gown. She groaned. *It's not supposed to be like this*, she thought, fighting back a wave of emotions welling up inside her. She had tried to end her life, and she had failed.

She balled her hands into tight fists, wondering how things had gone this far, when the door swung open and a doctor entered. He walked over to the bed and smiled down at her.

"Hi, Cathy! Nice to see you awake. I'm Dr. Robinson. How are you feeling?"

Looking up into his earnest face, Cathy found she had no idea how to answer his question.

He picked up her chart and looked it over, seemingly pleased by what he saw. "You had a lucky escape there, Cathy!"

She tried to smile, to make it seem like she was doing OK, but her face must have given her away.

"That bad, huh?"

The gentle compassion in his voice undid her—she bit her lip, trying to keep control, but before she knew it, a torrent of emotion was tumbling out of her. Days, weeks, months, years' worth of turmoil flowed out with her tears.

The doctor sat down and waited quietly until she managed to get the first words out.

"I should have just died. It would've been easier."

Dr. Robinson tilted his head and watched her interestedly, but didn't say anything.

"I just feel so... lost! My life is perfect, but all I feel is emptiness. I have a wonderful home, and I love my family, but... I just don't know. It doesn't seem to be enough," she whispered.

She'd never voiced the feeling to anyone like this—it didn't seem right to her that she should feel that way. So many people had less, how dare she be unhappy with all she had? The doctor didn't frown, or tell her she was being silly, or spoiled. He just nodded, as if he understood completely.

"Plus... I've been having these nightmares."

"Nightmares?" he prodded gently.

"Yes. I'm not sure what they mean, but it's like—I know this is going to sound crazy—I feel like I'm being buried alive. I'm just stuck, and I keep trying to move, but I can't! And I can't breathe! The terror is overwhelming, and I wake up in a panic."

"Stuck?"

"Yes. Stuck." She let out a long sigh. She couldn't believe she was telling someone all this.

"Cathy, you're definitely not alone in feeling this way. Many people find themselves in similar situations. They try everything they can to get themselves 'un-stuck,' as it were, but nothing seems to work."

"Exactly! I don't know what else there is left to try! I've been in therapy, I've tried yoga, and I've read every self-help book in my local bookstore, and then some! Nothing seems to work. I guess I thought this was the only way out." Cathy pushed a loose strand of hair off her face. She felt weak and drained.

"Would you be open to trying one more thing?"

She almost laughed. "Oh, I don't know. I don't think there's anything left to try!"

The doctor smiled, "Still, I would like to suggest that you speak to someone. His name is Seth, and I've sent patients to him when they've found themselves where you are now. He's helped them find a way out. He can show you how to approach life differently, and take a different path."

She raised an eyebrow. "And what path would that be?"

He shrugged. "That would be for you and Seth to work out, don't you think?" He smiled again. "Why don't I arrange for him to come to the hospital and have a chat with you? Would you be open to that?"

"Do I have a choice?" she asked wearily. This was what she hated about opening up to someone: they always thought they knew exactly what you needed, and she'd heard enough and tried enough to realize that this was rarely the case.

"Of course you have a choice! I have neither the capacity nor the desire to force you to do anything. However, I do feel that I would not be doing my duty if I didn't strongly recommend that you see him."

Cathy lay back in her bed and closed her eyes. It was true she was worn out and had lost faith long ago that anyone or anything out there held any answers for her. As little as she wanted to be disappointed one more time, something about the doctor piqued her curiosity.

"I don't know about this!" she protested. "It sounds strange! Approaching life a 'different way'? What does that even mean?"

"It means that there are other options available to you that you may not have tried. You probably don't even know they exist!"

"I don't know, Dr. Robinson. I'm going to have to think about it. I've tried so many things. Why would this be any different?"

He got up and stood at the foot of her bed, resting his hands on the railing. "Just answer this: Are you willing to give it a shot?"

Cathy took a deep breath. The emotion from earlier had faded, and she was back to feeling the way she had for a long time: numb. She couldn't find a reason to accept nor to refuse. "Sure," she said. "Fine. Whatever."

After a few days of rest, Cathy was starting to feel stronger. She was sitting up in her hospital bed, sipping a cup of tepid, tasteless tea, when she heard a knock on the door. She was expecting the nurse—she'd asked for more sugar—but instead a man she didn't know poked in his head.

Oh my God, it's the ghost of Steve Jobs, was Cathy's first thought, until the man stepped inside, and she got a better look at him. The shape of his face was different, but the resemblance was definitely there—she wondered if he got many comments about it. He had greyish hair and looked like he might be in his early 50s. He was casually dressed—chinos and a plain shirt—and his spectacles balanced perfectly on the tip of his nose. He smiled at her like they were old friends.

"Hi, Cathy! I'm Seth," he chirped.

"Hi," she said, shifting in her bed. She felt uncomfortable at the way she imagined she looked; she hadn't even looked in the mirror since that fateful morning in the bathroom.

"How are you feeling?"

I'm in hospital because I tried to off myself on my birthday! How the hell do you think I'm feeling? was what she wanted to yell. Instead, she just shrugged. "OK, I guess," she said meekly.

He smiled a wide, irritatingly cheerful smile and sat down in the chair next to her bed. "Dr. Robinson told me a little bit about you. Would you mind telling me some more?"

Cathy felt something inside her snap. "Just say what you came here to say!" she growled. "'You tried to kill yourself, and you belong in a lunatic asylum!' I know that's what you're thinking!"

"That's what you think?"

"Isn't it true?"

He shook his head, "Cathy, I'm not here to judge you. I can see why you thought suicide was your only way out. You're not the only one who feels that way."

She looked away from him, fidgeting with the edge of her blanket. This man had only been in her room for a couple of moments, but she felt like he did understand what she was going through.

The chair creaked as he leaned forward. "Tell me a little bit more about why you felt the need to take your own life," he said quietly.

How could she even answer that? She had no idea where to start, but knew she had to be honest with him.

"The truth is, I've been feeling trapped inside my own life. I don't know how to change it. I'm just stuck. I haven't been happy in a long time."

Seth nodded encouragingly. "Go on."

"I know it's crazy!" she wailed. "I have everything I dreamed of having, and all my friends tell me how perfect my life is!" She faltered; her throat was closing up, and she needed to breathe deeply to steady herself. "It's just... everything I thought would make me happy... it just hasn't. I have a nice house, a wonderful family, I have enough money, but... but just I don't feel happy. And I feel so guilty for feeling unhappy! How can someone have so much and feel so unfulfilled?" She wiped her eyes. "With everything I have, I *should* feel better. I shouldn't feel like life is so boring and meaningless. But I don't know what to do to be happy! I feel trapped! I feel like I'm faking it every time I smile at my children! What kind of mother am I?"

A nurse walked in—Lucy, the tall brunette who *did* understand how Cathy liked her tea—and both Seth and Cathy fell silent while Lucy took her blood pressure.

Cathy was grateful for the time it gave her to order her thoughts. When Lucy had gone, she whispered, "I just feel so empty."

Seth patted her hand gently. "It sounds like you thought that if you had the right ingredients—a husband, kids, house, and money—it would automatically make you happy. Is that right?"

"Well... yes," she answered slowly. That much was just common sense, wasn't it? "What I don't understand is, how come it didn't it work for me? It seems to work for everyone else."

"How do you know it works for everyone else?"

She almost rolled her eyes. "Just look around! There are a lot of people it seems to work for."

Seth gave her a gentle smile. "What if I told you that happiness has nothing to do with any of those things?"

"I don't know. I can't imagine what else would make me happy!"

He squeezed her hand, "*That* is what I'm going to help you discover. If you'll let me, of course. The question is: Are you willing to do whatever it takes to find joy and fulfillment in your life?"

"It depends on how hard it is," she said slowly. Doubt clouded her mind. "Look, I know that I almost ended everything, but I'm not willing to give up the things that are dear to me. I love my kids and my husband. I do realize how much they mean to me!"

"Who said anything about *giving things up*? The question is, are you willing *to do* whatever it takes to find joy? Would it matter how easy or hard the path would be if it got you where you wanted to go?"

"I have no idea! Yes. No! Maybe? I don't know!" Cathy covered her face with her hands. She felt like screaming.

"OK, let me ask you this: Do you prefer warm or cold climates?"

"*What?*" Cathy looked at Seth as though he was mad. "What does that have to do with anything?"

"Just answer the question," he said steadily.

She sighed. This guy was making her want to tear her hair out. "Warm," she said. "Definitely warm."

"Great! Let's say I was going to send you on an all-expenses-paid vacation to somewhere nice and warm. Just the climate you wanted. Would that excite you?"

"It depends what else would be there." she replied slowly. Seth was a complete lunatic—she was sure of it now—but it was probably best just to humor him.

"Fair enough," Seth pressed on, "but let's focus on the climate for now. Would the warm weather suit you?"

"Yes. Absolutely!"

"With no other questions about the weather?"

"No other questions."

"So once your experience meets what I call the 'bottom line'—in this case the weather—there'd be nothing else to complain about?"

Cathy nodded.

Seth pushed his glasses up his nose—he looked like a university professor earnestly making a point. "What I'm trying to get at is that it's important to define the 'bottom line' of what you want, and stick to that with no conditions attached."

Cathy mulled this over, pulling a thread loose from her blanket. "So… what you're saying is, if I define my 'bottom line' as, say, joy, nothing else comes into the equation? I'm not sure about this."

"Well, what are the promises of the path you're on now?" Seth asked her.

She looked away. "I don't know if there are any promises," she said quietly.

"The good news, Cathy, is that the path I'm proposing now comes with a promise." His voice was gentle. "The path you're on now will only get you more of what you have. The path I have in mind will show you what's been in your way— what *really* keeps you from what you want is your fear. In order to get what you want, you will have to confront those fears, head on, as you move forward."

Seth paused and Cathy looked up at him, wanting him to continue. He smiled at her. "At every turn, you will have to decide which is more important: playing it safe or getting what you want."

"Playing it safe or getting what I want?" Cathy repeated, more to herself than to Seth.

"Yes. For example, just now, I asked a simple question, and your first response was mistrust. Whatever shows up is what you need to deal with first. In this case, it's a trust issue. Mistrust is the first thing that stands in your way. That's not to say that there's never a reason to be mistrustful, but you were mistrustful without any reason. Do you see that?"

Cathy fidgeted with her sleeves. "But it's hard to trust you. I don't even know you! You could be trying to trick me, get me into a nuthouse!"

Seth smiled. "I understand what you're saying, Cathy. But my point here is that your mistrust wasn't based on a real threat. I never asked you to do anything—or to trust me, for that matter."

Cathy frowned. "Well, you did promise I would get what I wanted, didn't you? I don't just follow people... Especially down roads I don't know."

Seth nodded. "I am presenting you with an opportunity to see something really important. Are you at least open to that?"

Cathy realized her hands were shaking. She was afraid, but she knew that she didn't want to stay where she was any longer. Somehow, what Seth said rang true—if she carried on as she was, she'd only get more of the same. She knew that in her gut. It was probably part of why life had seemed so hopeless.

"I'm reluctant to commit to something I don't know much about," she eventually said. "What is this opportunity?"

"You've been looking to your kids, marriage, community, and all there is in your present life to bring you happiness. But it seems that doesn't work. I'm proposing you look somewhere else...."

"Where?" Cathy asked, cutting him off. She wished he'd just get to the point— reminding her of what didn't work, of how she'd failed, wasn't getting either of them anywhere.

"Well, there are two paths we can take in life, each feeding on the other. One is internal and the other is external. You have chosen the external journey, and you've found that it hasn't brought you happiness. So I think the first place to start is to look within yourself, and to find happiness there. I'm proposing an inner journey that will get you where you want to go."

"Inner journey?" Cathy asked, sitting up straighter.

He smiled. "Let's try an experiment. I want you to imagine going back to your old high school. How would you feel walking in?"

Cathy felt her lips curve into a smile, and she blushed when she met Seth's gaze.

"You're remembering good things, aren't you?" he asked.

She nodded.

"And those memories are causing you to feel happy?"

"Oh, yes. I met my husband in high school."

Seth smiled. "So, it's safe to say that you recreated those feelings just by thinking about your high school? Without actually having to go there?"

Cathy shrugged. "Sure, you could say that."

"So the feelings are inside of you, independent of the circumstances. The trigger here is merely thinking of your high school."

"Where are you going with this?" Cathy frowned. He made it sound so simple. Life wasn't like that—was he trying to say she should just pretend and think happy thoughts all the time?

He leaned forward a bit. "All I want you to understand at this point is that what you feel isn't necessarily dependent on the outside world. Imagine there are two rooms inside of you—metaphorically speaking, of course! One is the Happy Room and the other is the Sad Room."

She raised an eyebrow. "That sounds a bit odd."

"Hear me out. Imagine that every time you go in the Happy Room, you're happy, no matter what is happening. You could be in the Happy Room and find out that the world is ending, and you'd still feel happy! Alternatively, in the Sad Room, you'll feel sad regardless of what's happening around you."

Cathy tilted her head. "So, I could be in the Sad Room and find out I've just won the lottery and still feel sad? That sounds crazy!"

Seth laughed. "No, what's crazy is that you wouldn't know that being in the Sad Room was causing your sadness. You'd make up an excuse to explain why you feel sad."

She sighed. "Let me get this straight. You're saying that I would be sad because, I don't know, I would think my lottery winnings weren't enough to buy a really big house? That would be my excuse?"

"Exactly! Now you're getting it!"

Cathy frowned—she was getting tired of all this.

"Let's put it another way. Imagine your room is heated to the boiling point, and you bring an ice cube into it. What would happen to the ice cube?"

"It would melt, of course!"

"Right. What if that ice cube had a personality, and was determined not to melt? Would that stop it from melting?"

She laughed, "No, of course not!"

He nodded. "No amount of will power or determination would enable that ice cube to remain icy in that environment. The only way it could remain an ice cube is if it left that particular room. The same way you can make a choice to leave any one of your internal rooms!"

She bit her lip. "But is there any way I could feel anything else besides sadness in the Sad Room?"

Seth shrugged. "Yes and no. You could do all kinds of things like buy new furniture and have friends come by, so you could make yourself feel better for short periods. But in the end, it wouldn't matter. What you're failing to see is that in either room you'd experience life from that perspective. You'd have no choice. Over time, all your thoughts and perceptions would be determined by the room you were in."

"That sounds crazy. Why wouldn't I just leave the Sad Room?"

He grinned at her. "Great question. The thing is, when we're in these rooms, we get locked in them and forget about our ability to leave. Most of the time, we don't even realize we're *in* a room. We think, 'Oh well, that's just life!' And even if we're smart enough to figure out we're stuck somewhere, the influence of the room is great enough that it affects the way we think. On top of that, we spend most of our time trying to figure out why we feel this way!"

Cathy nodded slowly. She felt like she was starting to understand.

"Now, imagine that there's a fire in this room. What do you think you'd focus on?"

"Getting the hell out of there!" Cathy laughed.

"Exactly." He smiled. "Trying to figure out why we feel what we feel in these rooms is like being in a burning room and pondering what causes the fire. If you try and make sense of the room, you get stuck in it! The only way to get out of the room is to *stop* thinking about it and focus on the kind of room you want to move into. The more you think about your current room, the more you make of it, and it just gets bigger! Quite simply, all you need to do is step out."

"Quite simply?" She shook her head. "You make it sound so easy! How do I do that?"

He pushed his glasses up his nose and looked into her eyes. "This is where it gets tricky. If you study the room, you will get stuck in the room. If you think about the room, you will get stuck in the room. And if you develop a plan to get out of the room, you will get stuck in the room! Instead, you need to focus not on the room you're in, but on the room you *want to go to*."

Cathy sighed. Her head was starting to pound. She looked out the window and noticed a bird sitting on the sill, his beak opening and shutting as if he was laughing at her. She found herself feeling envy toward the little bird—if only her life could be as simple as his!

"That's why you need to have a 'bottom line,'" Seth said gently. "Or let's call it a vision of what you really want. Unless you have a more compelling reason to leave, you will always stay in that room. Instead of leaving, most people spend their time trying to make the rooms they live in comfortable."

She looked back at him. "So, if I've spent so much time and effort trying to make my room comfortable, why would I leave that room and go to another room I know nothing about?"

Seth nodded as if he'd expected her question. "Without proof, no one feels confident that what lies ahead will be better. And it might not be easy—who's to say there won't be a fire in the building and you'll have to hop through flames to get to the other room?"

Cathy raised an eyebrow. "Are you still trying to sell this idea to me?"

He smiled. "Cathy, all I want to know is if you are willing to take this journey and do anything to discover your 'bottom line.'"

She closed her eyes for a moment and tried to make sense of all Seth had said. A part of her wanted to run and hide, but she reminded herself of the desperation she had felt just a few days ago.

"I guess I could give it a go," she whispered nervously. "I have nothing else left to try. Maybe I *will* take this journey."

Seth smiled. "I'm pleased to hear it. The doctors say you'll be fit to go home in a few days. I'd like you to come into my office next Monday." He dipped his hand into his pocket and gave Cathy a business card. "I really look forward to taking you on this journey."

Cathy looked down at the card and then back up at Seth. For the first time in a long time, she smiled.

CHAPTER 2

The Journey

On Monday, Cathy woke up early and got ready to go see Seth. She couldn't remember the last time she'd felt so nervous. Even so, she felt a strange sense of determination—since she'd left the hospital, everyone had been tiptoeing around her, afraid of saying or doing the wrong thing. She didn't want this to be what her family life was like.

She found she couldn't stop thinking about what Seth had said. The more she thought about it, the more sense it seemed to make: happiness and sadness lay inside *her*, independent of circumstances. Sadness had become a very bad habit in her life. She'd become so used to it that it had become her home! *What a strange idea. Even if we're miserable, we can still call a place home!*

She was glad that she'd decided to make a change. Granted, she had no idea where she was going, and that terrified her. It was like going straight into the unknown! She knew this new place wouldn't feel like home at all, but she also knew she had to try *something*.

The address on Seth's card turned out to be a brownstone office building along a tranquil, tree-lined avenue. She parked her car and looked at herself in the rear-view mirror. *Am I really ready for this?* The Cathy in her reflection looked composed and clear-eyed. She winked at herself for luck, took a deep breath, and got out of her car.

A friendly receptionist let her in and asked her to take a seat in the waiting room. There were already two people sitting there—Cathy sat down and pretended to read a magazine, looking them over. Seated closest to the door was a tall, dark young man reading a car magazine. His long hair veiled his eyes. She looked over his baggy, ripped jeans and couldn't help thinking: *I hope my son never comes home looking like that!*

Sitting closer to Cathy was an older woman, dressed in what were clearly very expensive, designer clothes. Her hair was the perfect shade of blonde and looked perfectly, professionally done. In fact, the woman looked as if she had just stepped out of a beauty salon. She had beautifully manicured nails, and her make-up was artfully done.

Cathy shifted in her chair. Looking at the woman made her realize how much she had let herself go since she'd become a mother. It wasn't that she was unattractive, but she knew she could easily be described as a plain Jane. She seldom bothered with doing her hair and never wore make-up unless she absolutely had to. She flipped the page of her magazine, trying to hide her untidy fingernails, and made a half-hearted attempt to read.

After a few minutes, two more people arrived at the same time. A woman, probably in her mid-thirties, giggled as she tried to pass through the doorway at the same time as the man in front of her.

"I'm so sorry," she said, tugging down the hem of her loose-fitting t-shirt. She was slightly chubby and had bright pink cheeks. She seemed a little out of breath when she sat down opposite Cathy.

The man who came in with her looked like he was in his late forties and seemed relaxed. There was a designer label on his shirt, but he was also wearing faded blue jeans. His green eyes were sharp and alert, and his grey hair was cut short. *Nice looking,* Cathy thought, before mentally slapping herself on the wrist.

He'd just sat down and chosen a magazine from the stack on the table when another man walked in. He looked closer to Cathy's age, if not slightly younger. His hair was black with specks of grey, and his blue eyes gleamed as they scanned the room. His suit was perfectly tailored and impeccably smart. He caught her eye and smiled, revealing a set of perfect teeth.

He too took a seat, and Cathy looked back down at her magazine, continuing to turn pages without really reading. The people in the waiting room with her all seemed so different. Had any of them been where she was? She couldn't imagine the perfectly dressed woman or the man in the nice suit on the edge of desperation. Why had any of them needed to come to Seth?

The scruffy young man's watch beeped twice, making her look up—it was nine o' clock. Cathy took a deep breath, and right on cue, the inner door opened, and Seth came out of his office.

"Hey, everyone! Welcome!" he said in his usual, cheery manner.

They all rose and followed him into his office. It was airy and gorgeously lit, and the walls were lined with dark wood shelves crammed with books. Seth gestured to the elegant, luxurious sofas in the middle of the room, and they sat. The table before them was laden with coffee and muffins.

"Please, help yourselves," he said, smiling.

The muffins looked good, and the coffee smelled heavenly, but Cathy found she was too nervous to eat.

Seth poured himself a cup and sat down. "I've already met with you all individually, and I would like to welcome you again on your journey," he said. "I know you're all wondering where exactly this is all going to take place, and you'll probably be surprised to know it's going to happen in the room right next door!"

They all looked at one other, and Cathy was sure they were all thinking the same thing: *Is it too late to run?*

"Remember I said that this was going to be an 'inner journey'? That is true, but it's also going to be a virtual one. Technology has enabled us to do some wonderful things!"

"So where exactly will this journey take us?" asked the woman with the pink cheeks.

"Aha! Good question. Our objective is to know ourselves on the highest level possible. We call that level the Higher Self. It is already present in each one of us, so it's just a matter of coming to know it."

"How will we know when we get there?" Cathy asked.

Seth smiled. "You will know you're there when you reach the Stream."

A Journey to the Stream

"The Stream?" echoed the good-looking man with the green eyes.

Seth nodded. "Yes. The Stream is the place of ultimate joy and ultimate fulfillment. It is there that you will find everything you ever wanted, and more. Throughout your journey, you must focus on getting to the Stream."

Some of the people nodded at Seth in understanding. Cathy chewed her lip. *What if it was too hard?*

"In order to get to the Stream, you will have to pass through six towns," Seth continued. "There are no shortcuts: you have to go through each and every town before you can get there."

"Do we have to go together the whole way?" asked the man with perfect teeth.

"You *can* help each other, but it's not your focus. Some of you might get stuck along the way and find it difficult to leave a particular town, and that's when you'll have to decide individually whether to stay or whether to move on."

"How will we know which way to go?" the beautifully made-up woman asked.

"You'll work it out. It won't always be easy, but you'll work it out," Seth replied, smiling reassuringly. "But before we go any further, you should introduce yourselves to your fellow travelling companions. Let's start with you and go clockwise." He pointed to the young, scruffy man, who seemed to be studying his fingernails but after a moment noticed it was his turn, sat up and cleared his throat.

"Hi, guys. I'm Pedro, I'm 27 years old, and I work as a waiter. I'm here because I just haven't been able to figure out what I want to do with my life. I've just kind of been drifting around with no real direction. I'm hoping this process will help me get clear about it."

He shrugged to show that he was finished. Next to speak was the handsome one.

"Hi, everyone, I'm Richard. I'm 48 and I've been quite successful in business. I've come to realize my strategies have gotten me a lot of money, but have not led to me to real fulfillment. I always thought that money was the answer to everything, and once I had it, things would be great. But the funny thing is, now I feel just as empty, if not more so, than I did before. I'm hoping that Seth's program—this Stream thing—will help me break through whatever this roadblock is, and show me what more there is to life, besides money."

Seth nodded encouragingly. "Thanks, Richard. Next?"

"I'm Betty," said the perfectly made-up woman. "I'm 50, and I have two grown children. I am divorced, and I'm quite secure, financially. Since my divorce, I haven't really been doing much with my life. I'm not here because I have issues I want to solve, but because I feel like I have a calling for something greater in my life, and I don't seem to know what it is or how to get there. I've done everything I thought I was supposed to do, and I'm ready to discover something new."

"Great! Next?" said Seth, looking at Cathy.

She swallowed hard. "Hi, I'm Cathy. I'm 41 years old and married, with two kids. I recently had an… experience, which has made me realize that I need to make a change in my life. I have everything I've ever wanted, but I don't feel happy. I feel stuck, and I'm hoping that this journey will take me to the place of ultimate joy Seth talks about."

Next up was the last of the women. "I'm Janine," she said, giggling. "I'm 37 and single. I've never been able to find anyone to marry. All the guys I meet just never work out. I don't really have a career; every job I've started has gone sour for me sooner or later, and I've just moved on. I always feel so uncertain about the choices that I make. I'm here to see if I can find some clarity."

Seth nodded, "And lastly?"

"It's Bill," the man with the perfect teeth said. Cathy thought he looked out of place: he'd probably look more comfortable in a boardroom, telling people what to do. "I'm 39. To be honest, I'm not sure what I'm doing here. I love a challenge, so I guess that's why! I'm a self-made man. No one has helped me get where I am. I've worked in finance my whole life, and I've been very successful. Now I'm just trying to figure out what I want to do next."

"Thanks, Bill." Seth beamed at them. "Now that you're all better acquainted, let's get started!"

He led them to an adjoining room where there were several capsule-like devices lined up against the wall—they made Cathy think of tanning beds.

"Please, make yourselves comfortable," Seth said, gesturing toward the capsules. "These machines will allow you to go on your internal journey, so that you can face your fears and everything that holds you back from reaching the Stream, while your physical bodies remain completely safe in this room."

Cathy felt a flutter of excitement rippling through her stomach as she got into her capsule. She'd been so overwhelmed with nervousness that she hadn't even thought that this might be fun!

Seth walked around the group, making sure everybody was comfortable. Once everyone was settled, he sat down at the instrument panel. With the press of a few buttons, the doors of their capsules began to shut. A countdown to their journey began, and Seth's voice came through the earpiece: "Always remember and keep focused on your goal: Get to the Stream."

5…4…3…2…1…

CHAPTER 3

Beginning at the Beginning

The blackness slowly faded until suddenly there was too much light. Cathy found herself lying on her back on something that felt like grass, but had to wait for her eyes to adjust before she could see anything. When she sat up and looked around, blinking, she noticed her five travelling companions stirring beside her. They were in a sunny field, amid long grass. She could see a forest off in the distance.

"Where are we?" she asked, rubbing her eyes.

"Wherever we are, we need to make a plan to get to this Stream. I don't want to waste any time," said Bill, getting up.

She looked up at him. "I'm with you, but I think we should make sure everyone else is OK first."

He glared at her, but she ignored him and turned to the others. They were sitting up slowly, and everybody seemed unharmed, if a little disoriented.

"Should we try and find a map?" asked Richard.

"What, in the middle of nowhere? Good luck with that," Bill snorted.

"We should at least try," Richard retorted. "Seth wouldn't have sent us to a place with nothing, surely."

They all got to their feet and searched around for a map or any indicator that might guide them in the right direction, but—aside from an interesting-shaped rock Pedro spotted—nobody found anything.

"Alright then," said Bill, darting a told-you-so glance at Richard. "Let's start moving. There has to be a gas station along that road. They're bound to know the way."

Betty frowned. "I'm not so sure," she said. "I think we should wait here and see if someone shows up, then we can ask them the way. I don't want to walk for miles in the wrong direction. Or maybe we can try to find a cab." She turned to Pedro beside her. "What do you think?"

He'd been staring at his sneakers and didn't look up when she spoke. "Whatever. I don't care."

Betty leaned back a bit with raised eyebrows and scolded him, "That's really not helpful, Pedro!"

Cathy stepped forward, hands up. "Okay, okay. Let's not start our journey off with an argument. Betty, we need to get to the first town, and sitting around waiting isn't going to get us there any faster."

Before Cathy could finish her sentence, Bill had already started walking toward the road.

"Wait up!" she called, trying to herd the others together to start walking.

They'd walked a few minutes when Janine asked quietly, "Are you sure it's this way?" She was looking around nervously and frowning.

Richard raised an eyebrow. "Do you know something we don't?" he asked.

"Well, no. Not really. But I have a feeling it's the other way," she said, pointing over her shoulder.

Cathy turned, but she couldn't make out much that way, just what looked like a building of some sorts. She couldn't really tell what kind.

"And what are you basing this 'feeling' on, Janine?" asked Bill with irritation, his hands on his hips. He'd stopped walking, and the others had managed to catch up with him.

She shrugged. "I just have a good feeling about these kinds of things."

"That sounds crazy. You've never even been here before! At this point, one way is just as good as any other."

"Look, none of us know the way," said Cathy. "If Janine says she has a good feeling about that way, I think we should listen to her. Is everyone else OK with that?"

"Sounds fine," said Betty.

Richard nodded, and Pedro shrugged his shoulders.

"Hey, you guys don't have to listen to me," said Janine, holding her hands up defensively. "If you want to go this way, we can go this way. But somehow I just *know* it's the other way."

Bill threw up his hands. "Well, why didn't you just say that in the first place?" he asked, sounding exasperated.

"I did, you just didn't listen to me!"

They turned around and started walking in the opposite direction. Just when Cathy started to feel like things might be looking up, Janine said quietly, "I just hope I don't get blamed if it's not the right way."

Bill glared at her. "Am I in a dream or a nightmare? Because right now I feel like I'm in hell!"

"It's OK, Bill," said Cathy, trying to calm him down. "We're off to the Stream, remember? Let's be happy. We've got to work together!"

He scoffed. "Whatever."

"Janine," Cathy said, turning to her travel companion, "You had a good feeling about this way, right?"

"Well... I mean, I didn't say I was *sure*..."

"Hold on a moment. Now she says she's not sure? You've got to be kidding me!" Bill's face began to take on a dangerous tinge of purple around the edges.

"It's just... I hope I'm right!" Janine looked down at her shoes. "Maybe we should turn back." Her voice was almost inaudible.

"That's what I wanted to do in the first place!" Bill growled. "Janine, if you change your mind one more time..."

"Janine, are you sure this time?" Richard asked sternly.

She nodded.

"We're on our way now!" Cathy said cheerfully, trying to keep the peace. "Let's just turn around and see if that leads us to the first town."

After walking for an hour, they were all hot, tired, and desperate for something to drink. They were struggling up a hill when Betty gasped, "A gas station! Look, over there!"

Cathy caught Betty's eye, and they grinned at each other like little children. Everyone seemed energized now—they whooped and cheered and started moving faster. And, Cathy noted, with more spring in each step.

Richard was the first to reach it. They couldn't see his face, but his loud, colorful swearing made Cathy's heart sink. "It's closed!" she heard him shout.

"This is strange," said Bill, when they'd all made it there. "The sign says, *Closed— Opening Soon—Will Let You Know*. What the hell does that mean?"

Cathy came around to read it, hardly believing her ears. "That's odd," she said. It didn't make any sense—not to mention how unprofessional it seemed.

"And how do they plan to 'let us know'?" asked Betty. "I've travelled all over the world, and I've never seen such a thing!"

"That's just the way some people are, I guess," said Pedro, making Cathy jump. He didn't open his mouth that often. "No worries, let's just keep going."

"Maybe we should wait!" Janine piped up. "I have a feeling they'll open in a little while."

Bill rolled his eyes. "Here we go again with another one of your 'hunches'. How can you be so sure?"

"Stop it, Bill! How do you know they won't be opening soon?"

"Because I have common sense, you idiot!"

Janine gasped. "How dare you speak to me like that?"

"Man, everyone needs to chill out," said Pedro, shaking his head. "What's the big deal anyway?"

"Pedro's right!" Cathy cut in, before the arguing could start again. "Bill, there's no need to be so rude," but he shook his head and turned away, making her want to shake him. "And Janine," she continued. "With all due respect, this sign looks like it's been here for a while. I don't think they're going to be opening any time soon. I think we should keep moving."

"So you're taking his side now?" Janine complained, looking hurt.

"Ugh! I can't take this anymore!" Bill started to walk away. "Do what you want, I'm going."

Cathy turned to follow him, glancing over her shoulder at the others as she did. Richard shrugged and set off after her, and Betty and Pedro followed. When they'd reached Bill, they heard running footsteps behind them—Janine caught up and grudgingly fell into step with them.

"I just think it'll open soon if we wait," she muttered.

Betty stopped, frowning. "Maybe she has a point," she said.

Cathy wasn't sure whether to scream or to cry. It was hot, she felt sticky and sweaty from all the walking, and she was thirsty—she'd never looked forward to a drink of water this much in her entire life. She turned around to face Janine and Betty and said, "Everyone else agrees that we should keep moving. Is that OK with you two?"

"Who put you in charge?" said Betty, spitefully. "I think waiting would be better."

Janine shrugged. "Whatever," she muttered. She was starting to sound like an insolent child.

Cathy was fighting the urge to order both women into time out when Richard spoke up. "If there's one thing we can agree on, it's that we need to find a place to eat and sleep before the sun goes down. We're bound to find the first town soon, so I strongly suggest we keep walking."

Cathy could have hugged him. Betty and Janine looked at each other and hurried past Cathy to catch up with the others.

CHAPTER 4

After two hours of walking, the travelers came across a signpost that read, *Either Way*. Cathy didn't think she'd ever seen a more unhelpful sign; both sides tapered off into arrows, so the sign seemed to point in opposite directions.

"This is just ridiculous," Bill muttered.

"What do we do now?" Betty sounded panicked, and Cathy found she couldn't really blame her.

There was a tall, old tree nearby, and Cathy sat down on one of the roots, thankful for the rest and cool shade. The others followed suit, settling near her, and they collectively pondered the useless signpost in silence.

Quite unexpectedly, Janine snapped her fingers and sat a little straighter, "I think we should take the path to the right!" she declared.

Inwardly, Cathy rolled her eyes. She didn't want to take any more directions from Janine.

"That's it. I've had enough of this nonsense!" Bill fumed. He leapt to his feet and stomped off by himself. Cathy realized she wasn't even worried about getting separated anymore; she'd come to realize Bill just needed to let off steam sometimes and would be back on his own, but it wasn't long before they heard him shout, "Hey, guys! There are buildings over there! That must be the first town!"

Cathy jumped up and sped off in the direction of Bill's voice. When she reached him, he beamed at her and pointed to what he'd seen.

She gasped. "Yes, I see them too!" she cried, unable to contain her excitement.

The others had caught up, and she couldn't help grinning at them. "I think we're almost there!"

After a few minutes of walking—it might have been five, it might have been thirty, but Cathy was too excited to care—they made it to the town square. She felt ready to kiss the ground. It was a cute little town—all the buildings seemed to be designed in different styles. The mismatch and clash of colors was charming.

"Look at that!" Janine exclaimed, pointing.

Cathy followed her gaze. There were about a dozen signs above the Town Hall, but each one was painted over in black, so Cathy couldn't make out what they might have said. The only sign not obliterated said *Either Way Town Hall*. It seemed brighter than all the others; she had the feeling it was very newly painted.

"The sign post outside the town makes sense now," Bill observed.

'Either Way' seemed a strange name for a town, but it was a mystery she would ponder later. For now, all she could think about was finding a hot shower and a warm bed. There were several hotels in sight, and, no surprise to Cathy, her fellow travelers began to disagree over where to stay.

"Let's stay at Maple Lodge!" cried Janine, pointing excitedly. "Look, they have a spa! I've got a good feeling about this place."

"No way," Bill said firmly. "I think we should stay at Oak Ridge. *They* have free Wi-Fi."

"Oh, Bill, let's not get into this again," said Cathy. "It doesn't really matter where we stay, as long as there's a shower and a bed!"

"How about this place?" asked Richard, pointing to a pale yellow building. "It looks comfortable and reasonably priced. Granted, the name is a bit strange—*Your Place or Mine*. But they have a pool, air conditioning, *and* free Wi-Fi."

Betty giggled. "That *is* a strange name, but you're right about it looking like a good choice," she said.

"That one looks good," said Pedro, gesturing to something over Cathy's shoulder.

She turned around to see a building that looked like a wooden shed, painted pale blue. *Not exactly luxurious,* she thought.

"Are you out of your mind?" she heard Betty gasp. "The windows are filthy!"

"And there's no way they have Wi-Fi," Bill added.

Another argument began, and Cathy tuned them out, looking around. She realized that many of the shops, and even some of the hotels, had signs outside similar to the ones they'd seen above the Town Hall: lots of information scratched out, or many new posters tacked on over old ones.

Cathy noticed a familiar face leaving the Maple Lodge and walking toward the group—Janine. She hadn't even realized the girl had walked away. Cathy sighed. She wished Janine would be more considerate.

"Yeah, I'm not so sure about that one," Janine told them. "I think we should go with *Your Place or Mine*."

Bill rolled his eyes. "Here you go again with the indecision! I've had enough! Not to mention we've only just started this journey! You really get to know a person when you travel...."

"Bill, that's enough!" Cathy interrupted. "I am exhausted and sick of all this bickering! Let's just check into a hotel. Any hotel! I hardly care at this point!"

She spoke more harshly than she had intended to, but it did have the desired effect—the bickering stopped. Some of them even nodded agreement.

"Yeah, dude," said Pedro, "I could use a beer. I hope there's a mini bar."

Richard smiled. "Guess that's decided then."

There *was* a mini bar in the room, as it turned out. Along with beer, it also had grape juice—Cathy's favorite. She downed the bottle in what seemed like one long gulp, and then showered for twice as long as she usually did; the hot water and beautifully scented soap felt like the highest of luxuries. Knowing a warm, inviting bed would be waiting for her afterward made it feel that much better. She slipped under the covers, and made a mental note never to take her bed at home for granted ever again. Or her husband. The hotel bed felt a little too big: aside from her stay at the hospital, Cathy hadn't slept alone in years.

She smiled. She felt eager to see what *Either Way* was all about, so they could understand it and move on to the next town. She was there to find some answers, she reminded herself as she drifted off, feeling very good about her decision to take this journey.

At breakfast the next day, her fellow travelers looked every bit as refreshed as Cathy felt. She was happy to see everyone relaxed and good-humored, happily discussing breakfast food. It made a welcome change from all the bickering.

"I think I'll have the eggs," said Bill. He frowned. "Well… maybe I'll have the pastries." He looked perplexed.

"What's wrong, Bill?" Cathy asked.

He shook his head. "It's really weird! I don't usually find it this hard to make up my mind! Especially when it comes to breakfast."

Cathy looked the menu over. "Wow, this looks great! There's a cooked breakfast with eggs and bacon!" She paused. There was also a Continental-style breakfast with pastries, bread, and cheese. She found she couldn't decide what she wanted to eat, either.

Nobody seemed to know what they wanted—when the waiter came over, they had to ask him to give them a few more minutes to decide. Eventually they did order—Cathy went for the cooked breakfast—and Janine was the last to go. After a few moments of frowning at the menu she said, "You know what, I'm not really hungry. I think I'll just have a coffee."

"Janine, we've got a big day ahead of us. You really should eat something," Cathy told her.

"I can't! I just don't know what to choose!"

"It's just breakfast! Order something! Anything!" Bill said, sounding exasperated.

But Janine just shook her head and asked the waiter to bring her a black coffee.

"With milk on the side!" she shouted after him.

When the food arrived, Richard looked at the waiter sheepishly. "I'm really sorry, but I've changed my mind. Could I have the cooked breakfast with scrambled eggs, please? No, wait. Make them fried!"

The waiter seemed unfazed and returned a few minutes later with Richard's eggs.

Janine giggled and told him, "And you can take the milk back. I don't want it anymore."

Once they'd eaten, they began to discuss their plans for the day.

"I think we should split up. Might be the best way to find out what this town is all about," said Bill, wiping his mouth with a napkin.

"Is that really such a good idea?" asked Betty. "I think we should stick together. We don't want to get lost in a place we don't know!"

"*I'm* only too happy to go it alone," said Janine, agreeing with Bill for once.

"Good plan," said Bill. "I don't want the rest of you questioning my directions every step of the way!" he said, looking sideways at Janine.

"Betty, why don't you and I stick together?" said Cathy. She didn't really feel like exploring the town on her own.

They agreed to meet back at the hotel for lunch, then went their separate ways.

At lunchtime, they gathered in the lobby of the hotel, but Janine appeared to be running late.

"Does anyone know where Janine is?" Cathy asked.

"I saw her earlier chatting to some locals in the park," Richard told them. "She seemed quite engaged in conversation, so she could be a while."

"Let's just eat without her."

Cathy wasn't surprised that this idea had come from Bill.

"Good idea," said Betty. "I'm starving!"

"I really think we should wait for her," said Cathy. She looked Bill straight in the eye. "I know I'd hate it if the rest of you went ahead and ate without me."

But Bill was already walking towards the restaurant, with Betty and Pedro in tow.

Richard turned to her. "We can't wait for her every step of the way. She'll catch up," he said kindly. "Let's just have lunch in the meanwhile."

Cathy sighed. "I just can't stand Bill's impatience. We're all in this together, and I wish he'd be a little more sensitive sometimes."

They joined the others at a table by the window just as Bill was placing his order.

"I'm having the steak!" he proclaimed. "Medium-rare."

"I'll have a pizza," said Pedro, before adding, "Or maybe not. Hold on. Maybe I'll have a burger." He stared at the menu. "No, I'll stick to the pizza," he confirmed.

After they'd deliberated for a few more minutes—and also called the waiter back several times to change their orders—Cathy sank back in her chair and sighed. She felt tired—she wasn't sure whether it was the long trek the previous day messing with her system, but making decisions had been difficult and draining for her all day.

On Cathy's right, Betty closed her menu and got up, moving to sit at the opposite side of the table. Cathy didn't think much of it at first; she figured maybe Betty wanted more sun. But when the food arrived, Betty moved her plate and went back to Cathy's side of the table. She took a few bites and then stopped suddenly, looking irritated, and picked her plate up and marched over to the other side again.

"What are you doing?" Richard asked, with interest.

Betty huffed. "I can't decide which way I want to sit! I think it's best to have the sun behind me, but when I sit that way, I think it may be best to have the sun in front of me!"

Cathy caught Richard's eye and raised a brow. He gave her a discreet shrug in response.

They continued eating in silence. As silly as Betty's shenanigans seemed, Cathy found she could relate to them. Perhaps the long walk had disoriented them all. Or maybe….

She gasped, dropping her fork. "Maybe it's this town!"

Her companions looked at her blankly.

Cathy sipped her drink, trying to collect her thoughts. "When I was walking in the town center, I found out some interesting things. The town is politically split: one half is conservative, and the other is very liberal."

"What's so interesting about that?" asked Bill. "Sounds like the whole USA."

She shook her head. "Not quite," she told him. "Because of the split, they can't make their minds up about anything! One election the conservatives get in and implement one set of policies. Then the next election the liberals come in and undo everything the conservatives have done!"

"They'll never get anything done that way," Richard commented wryly.

"Is that why they can't decide on a name for the town?" Pedro asked.

"Exactly!"

"Gosh, that sounds exhausting!" said Betty.

Cathy had to stifle a laugh—Betty was halfway through walking to the other side of the table again.

They finished their meals slowly, discussing the different things they'd seen and heard that day, and were drinking coffee when Janine finally walked in.

"Sorry I'm late," she breathed. "I'm famished!" She motioned to the waiter to bring her a menu.

Cathy studied her. She seemed flushed, but didn't look particularly sorry. "Janine, where have you been?" Cathy asked.

"Oh, it's no big deal," Janine responded, opening her menu and scanning it.

The other travelers looked at one other.

"Janine," said Bill, eyeing her levelly. "Where the hell have you been?"

She dropped her menu and glared at him. "What's it to you?" she retorted.

"We were worried about you," Cathy interjected, before they had *another* blow up, and now Janine at least had the grace to look embarrassed. "We've been discussing the things we noticed about this town. Do you have any insights to share?"

Janine fidgeted with her menu. "It's a long story," she said, not meeting Cathy's gaze.

Cathy glanced at Bill, who rolled his eyes. "We have time," she told Janine.

"Okay, okay!" Janine sighed. "I... I met a guy in the park, and we hung out! I really like him!"

Cathy felt her stomach drop. *Uh-oh.*

"You 'really like' a guy you've just met? Are you insane?" Bill snorted.

Janine scowled at him. "Stop picking on me! You're such an asshole, Bill."

"Okay, guys, cool it," Richard inserted, shooting Bill a look to keep him quiet. "Go on, Janine. What happened?"

She glared at Bill before softening and continuing. "Well, he's really smart and funny. I was having a really good time!" She looked at Cathy. "Sorry to have worried you," she said, looking genuinely apologetic.

Before anyone else could comment, Janine called the waiter over and ordered fish and chips. Several seconds later, she called him back and changed her order to a tuna salad.

Bill looked at the other travelers, appearing to ignore Janine completely. "OK, gang. I think we need to focus on getting to the Stream."

They nodded and made noises of assent, but Janine said, "Sure thing. Let's do it next week."

"Next week? I want to leave tomorrow!" Bill exclaimed. "Why hang around here?"

"I can't leave," said Janine quietly, looking down at her lap.

"What do you mean *can't*? Why *can't* you?" Bill's annoyance was obviously growing—the veins on his forehead started to swell.

"I told Jim I'd stick around for a while."

"Jim? Is that the guy from this morning?"

"Yes."

"You've lost your mind for sure! You want to stay in some strange town just so you can hang out with some guy you've just met?"

"Look, Janine, I don't want to get into your business, but this is affecting everyone. We want to get to the Stream... remember the Stream?" said Richard.

"Yes, so? What's the rush? I want to get there, too, but it'll still be there next week!"

Cathy looked Janine in the eye and said as gently as she could manage, "Janine, I understand that you like this guy, but you've only just met. What do you think is going to happen? Do you think there's a future with him?"

"Yes! Definitely!" She looked away. "Well... I think so. I hope so."

Out of the corner of her eye, Cathy saw Bill shake his head in exasperation.

"There's just... one small hiccup," Janine went on. She looked sheepish. "He's... He's actually engaged."

"Engaged?" Bill echoed incredulously. "Are you out of your fucking mind? Why are you chasing someone who's unavailable?"

Janine looked hurt. "What's the big deal? They haven't set a date yet! He's not going to marry her."

"Ah," said Richard softly. He put his hand on Janine's. "What gave you that impression? How long has he been engaged?"

"What is this, 20 questions? Mind your own business!"

"Janine, please," Cathy begged. "We've got to help each other get to the Stream, remember? We're only trying to help."

She chewed her bottom lip. "It's not like it's that serious of an engagement. I don't know why this is such an issue."

"How long has he been engaged?"

Janine stared down at her hands. "15 years."

"15 years!?" Bill exploded. "Now I'm *convinced* you're insane! I can't believe I got stuck on this trip with a fucking lunatic!"

"Bill, that's enough!" said Richard, raising his voice.

Bill looked away, shaking his head.

"Janine, I know it's hard for you not being married, but do you really think he's going to break off his engagement after 15 years?" Betty asked as kindly as she could.

"I agree with Betty, Janine. Things like this seldom work out for the best. How old is Jim, anyway?" Cathy asked her.

"What's wrong with you guys? Why are you being so judgmental?" Janine glared at them. "I've been searching for *the one* my whole life, and now I've finally found him. Can't you just be happy for me? You're all starting to get on my nerves!"

Something about Janine's defensiveness made Cathy's skin prickle. "How old is he, Janine?" she pushed on, as gently as she could.

Janine raised her chin defiantly. "He's 60."

Cathy tried to keep her expression neutral, but her companions didn't seem to be trying as hard; they stared at Janine in outright horror.

"It's not that bad!" Janine cried. "I'm 37, and I've always gone for older guys anyway." She smiled brightly—too brightly, in Cathy's opinion. "More experienced, if you know what I mean," she said, winking at Betty.

"Janine, 15 years seems kind of a long time for an engagement," said Richard patiently. "But for a guy who's 60, it seems *very* long. What is he waiting for?"

She shrugged. "It's not that odd here. Everyone takes their time before they get married. Almost everyone here is engaged."

The waiter brought Janine's salad and she started to pick at it, not really eating.

"That seems a little bit strange, don't you think?" Cathy asked. "I'm all for long engagements—I was engaged for two years before I got married—but in the end, I actually did get married. Why do you think everyone here is still engaged?"

"They just haven't made up their minds yet. And as long as he's not married, I feel sure that he'll break off his engagement and propose to me! I'm not leaving Either Way before he does. I've been waiting so long for the right guy to come along, and I know he's the one!"

The group fell silent—probably nobody knew what more there was to say, Cathy thought. She felt bad for Janine. While she could understand the girl's enthusiasm, Cathy had a bad feeling about the situation. She was sure it would end in heartbreak.

Across the table from her, Betty smacked her forehead. When Cathy looked at her, surprised, she laughed. "I think I've got it!" she told them. "It's so obvious! Everyone here is so indecisive and uncertain about *everything*. No wonder I can't decide which way to sit, and none of us can decide what to order. No one here can make up their minds about anything, and it's rubbing off on us!"

Cathy gasped. It sounded so simple, but it made so much sense. The countless painted-over signs above the town hall, the impossibly long engagements, the political stalemate—of course!

"I think you're right, Betty. That makes perfect sense. No wonder we're always bickering and can't agree on anything!" said Richard.

"I think we can thank Bill for that," muttered Janine, looking at him with disgust.

Cathy shook her head. "No, can't you see?" she asked. "We're influenced by this place. There's something about this town that's causing us to be this way!"

Bill looked thoughtful. "You know, that makes a lot of sense. And it explains why I was so indecisive about my eggs this morning. It's been bothering me all day!"

"You're still an asshole," Janine grumbled. "This doesn't change anything."

"Oh, wake up, Janine!" Bill sighed. "This Jim guy's never going to make up his mind as long as he's stuck in this town...."

"No! Don't you 'wake up, Janine' me! It's not like that at all! And I'm sick of the whole lot of you!" Janine leapt up and grabbed her purse. "I have to get back to Jim. I *know* he's going to break off his engagement! In fact, I'm sure he's done it already. Screw all of you!" Janine slammed her chair into the table and stormed off.

"Wow, she totally, like, freaked out," said Pedro, chuckling quietly.

Cathy sighed, ignoring Pedro's comment. "How are we ever going to get to the Stream if we can't even get through lunch together?" she wondered aloud.

"You know what I think?" Bill tapped the table. "This is the town of *Ambivalence!*" he announced, smiling smugly at them.

"That's it! This town's definitely *Ambivalence!*" said Richard. He shook his head. "And the scary thing is how easy it is to get roped in and caught up in it."

Cathy looked at the people in the restaurant. *No wedding rings*, she noted. She sighed. "You can say that again."

Cathy lay back in her bed, sighing deeply. After Bill had had his epiphany, and Janine had stormed off, they tried to plan their next move. But they all just kept second-guessing their decisions and opinions, and couldn't agree on what to do next. Before they knew it, it was evening, and they were still debating.

Still, they had finally agreed on one thing: they all desperately wanted a good night's rest.

She wondered about this strange town and its constant state of uncertainty. No one seemed to be able to make up his or her mind. No one ever really managed to reach a firm decision about anything. Everyone was stuck! Their behavior was irrational and frustrating, and it kept them stuck, chasing unattainable goals!

Cathy fell asleep with one thought in her mind—they had to leave this place of *Ambivalence* before it rubbed off on them too much and they got stuck here forever!

The next morning, the five travelers gathered in the restaurant for breakfast and reminded each other to make clear and assertive decisions about what to order.

"We don't want a repeat of yesterday," Cathy laughed.

"And we need to plan a way forward and get out of this town before we get caught up in another useless debate," Richard added.

Cathy kept looking around, hopeful that Janine would join them, but there was no sign of her.

The biggest sticking point was what they would do about her. They were all—miraculously—in agreement about wanting to leave, and the sooner the better, but they couldn't agree on whether or not to wait for Janine.

"She's clearly taken by this guy, and this town. It's going to be hard for her to walk away," said Betty.

"Don't we owe it to her to wait for her?" Cathy asked. She knew she would feel guilty about leaving her behind.

"Let's give her a chance," said Richard. "We'll tell her that we want to move on to the next town tomorrow, and hope she decides to join us."

"Man, I hope she does. This place is too confusing to get stuck in," Pedro said, shaking his head.

Bill slammed his palm against the table. "I say we go and find her right now and *tell* her that we want out of this place as soon as possible!"

"Sounds like a plan," said Pedro, getting to his feet.

Cathy looked at Betty, who shrugged and followed suit. Richard smiled at her and got up too.

Cathy sighed inwardly. She didn't think Janine would like this.

They paid for breakfast and headed off. As they walked through the town, Cathy noticed the abundance of jewelry stores and the many large ads in their windows for engagement rings. *Figures*, she thought, smiling to herself.

When they reached the main square, they found Janine sitting alone in a coffee shop.

"Hey, guys!"

"Hey, Janine! What are you up to?" asked Cathy.

"Oh, I'm waiting for Jim. We have a coffee date but he seems to be running late," she said, fiddling with a packet of sugar that was lying on the table.

Cathy felt herself frown. Were people really so indecisive they couldn't bother to be on time?

"Janine, we need to talk to you. We're all ready to leave Either Way, and we would really like you to join us," Richard said warmly.

Janine looked at them, her face strangely blank. Cathy felt another surge of pity for her.

"He's definitely going to break off his engagement...," Janine said softly. "Soon! I just have to stick around. Perhaps in a few days, and then maybe Jim can come with me!" she said excitedly. "I'm sure I can convince him to come with us once *we're* engaged!"

"Remember the Stream! That's the place we have to reach," Cathy reminded her.

But Janine just shook her head.

There was obviously no moving her: Cathy turned to the others. "Maybe we can wait a few more days for her?"

"No way," said Bill. "We're leaving *today*, with or without her."

Cathy looked at Richard, imploring. He sighed.

"Janine, you have to learn this lesson yourself," he said. "We can't learn it for you. We have to move on." He looked at Janine with sympathetic eyes. "You do understand that, right?"

Janine nodded, smiling, but Cathy thought her eyes looked sad. The spirit of indecisiveness had definitely taken over; the poor girl was well and truly trapped in *Ambivalence*.

"It's fine!" Janine told them. "Don't feel bad about leaving me behind. I'll be fine." She smiled at them. "Go! Find the Stream! I already have what I've been looking for. Next time you see me, I might have an engagement ring on my finger," she said, winking.

The five travelers walked back to the hotel to gather their things, and began the journey out of Either Way.

As they reached the outskirts, Cathy looked behind her at the town they were leaving. She felt very relieved to be getting out of *Ambivalence*, but she couldn't help feeling sad for Janine. She could be here another 15 years, waiting for Jim to make up his mind. The thought made Cathy's heart break.

She turned back to her companions. Bill was walking in front, like always, and Betty and Pedro seemed involved in animated conversation. Richard's face was full of excitement, and he gave her a warm smile. She couldn't help returning it. They would find the Stream, she remembered. And she looked forward to the promise of what it had to offer.

CHAPTER 5

Faraway

As they trudged along, the landscape began to change. The sun was scorching, burning their skin, and the soil was dry and cracked. Cathy imagined it was what Mars must be like.

"What the hell is this?" Bill groaned. "It must be some kind of a joke."

"Maybe we're supposed to die here," chuckled Pedro.

Bill glared at him. "Thank you for that, Pedro. You rarely speak, but when you do, it's so uplifting!"

Pedro rolled his eyes. "Lighten up, dude! You're way too serious."

"*Alright*, guys!" Cathy burst in, exasperated. "Let's not start with this. I thought we left bickering behind in *Ambivalence!*"

The two men gave each other a dirty look, but didn't say any more, and walked on in grumpy silence.

Cathy sighed. Part of her still ached about leaving Janine behind. It might be just her imagination, but it felt like she could *hear* the silence where the young woman's footsteps should have been. Maybe it would have been better to let the men bicker, to cover up the lack of sound.

"Hey, guys," Pedro called, breaking Cathy's reverie. "That looks like something," he said, pointing to a large wooden signpost sticking crookedly out of the ground. He leaned close, squinting at it. "But I can't make out what it used to say."

Richard moved forward to study the sign, then shook his head. "It's too badly faded to read." He turned to the rest of the group. "Still… Even if we can't read what it says, there must be *something* nearby!"

Cathy looked around. She agreed with Richard—surely there wouldn't be a signpost here if there was nothing for it to point to? But looking around, she could see *nothing*. They were surrounded by bare, dry ground. She couldn't imagine anything living or even growing here, never mind a town.

Cathy shook her head. "This seems really weird. There's absolutely nothing here! Let's just keep walking."

Another half-hour of walking—and another half-hearted argument—and they finally came across another sign.

"*Faraway*," Pedro read. "That must be the name of next town."

"Let's hope so," said Richard, as they set off in the direction the sign pointed. "I'm getting pretty tired of walking."

"Tell me about it," Cathy muttered. *What I wouldn't give for a nice foot rub!* she thought.

"*Faraway* seems an odd name," said Betty slowly. She frowned. "I think we need to keep it in mind. Last time the name was a big clue."

"That's a good point," agreed Cathy. "But *Faraway*? What could that mean?"

"Maybe it's far away from everything else?" reasoned Richard.

"Don't be ridiculous!" groused Bill. "Nothing is ever that simple!"

"Quit being such a pain in the ass, Bill," said Richard matter-of-factly. "We're all eager to find out what the next town is about."

"Yes, but maybe we're wasting our time trying to make meaning out of something that *has* no meaning."

Richard frowned, "We were led here for a reason, right? It has to mean something. Otherwise, what's the point?"

Bill—walking as usual in front—looked back over his shoulder at Richard. "Maybe that *is* the point! We're always trying to create meaning where there isn't any—maybe this is just *nothing*!"

"But I can't conceive of *nothing*," said Betty, looking confused.

"Okay, you guys are totally flipping out now," said Pedro. "Chill out."

Bill made no sign of having heard him, and turned around to face the group. "But here's the proof ! We've arrived in the middle of nowhere—the middle of nothingness—and just listen to us trying to make something out of it!"

"Okay, Bill," said Cathy, stepping between him and Richard. "I think I can get my mind around the idea of nothingness. But what's the value in it?" she asked.

"You see, there you go again, trying to make something out of it! Maybe, by seeing nothing, we get to *really* see that we *invent* meaning. In reality, that meaning doesn't exist. I think this place's job is to help us drop the idea of meaning, so we can see clearly." He started walking again, and they all followed.

Cathy drew level with him, so she could see his face while they talked. "So you're saying the meaning we put on things distorts reality?"

He shook his head. "What I'm saying is, the fact that there is no meaning *doesn't mean anything*. We're imposing meaning where there is none because we're too concerned with creating meaning in things."

Cathy frowned. "Well, who wants a life without meaning?"

"Exactly my point. That's precisely why we try to create meaning where there is none."

"I think you've all got heatstroke," Pedro piped up from the back. "You're starting to sound like crazy people."

"Look!" Cathy cried out, pointing to a large sign on the horizon. "It says *Welcome to Faraway*! We must be here!"

"Then what on earth was that back there?" asked Richard.

"Nothing, I guess," said Bill, chuckling softly.

It was already dusk when they reached *Faraway*, all of them overheated and desperate for a cold drink and some solid rest.

"This town makes me feel like I'm in an old Western," said Richard, looking around.

Cathy had to agree; the place was dusty and quiet, and seemed rather underpopulated.

"I wouldn't be surprised to see some tumbleweed blowing past," added Pedro.

They walked up the main street toward the town square in search of a hotel.

"This one will have to do," said Cathy, pointing to a large, decrepit building—it was the only hotel in sight, and she was too tired to keep looking.

"But look at those smashed windows!" Betty gasped. "And it doesn't look like any lights are on. It seems really eerie, not my kind of place at all!"

"Sign says it's got 5 stars," said Richard, sounding surprised.

"And it's open for business, so we may as well have a look," said Cathy.

"I agree. It's too late to find anywhere else. Let's spend the night here and see if we can find somewhere else tomorrow," said Bill.

"Yeah, *if* we get out of it alive," Pedro added drily.

They ignored him and went inside, agreeing to meet in the hotel bar for a drink after settling into their rooms.

The exterior of the hotel hadn't done much to impress Cathy, but her room positively shocked her: there was a mat on the floor, and nothing else. There weren't even any windows. She left the room in a hurry, shut the door behind her, and met the others in the bar.

"I'm really not sure about this place," she said wearily. "How are we supposed to get any rest on a yoga mat on the floor?"

"I know," agreed Richard, looking as tired as she felt. "But it's just for one night. Let's try our best."

"Do you think maybe this is the third town, and whatever was back there was the second?" asked Betty, shifting to get comfortable on a hard, creaky chair.

Bill took a sip of whisky. "If that's true, we're making great progress."

"But it couldn't have been. None of us even came close to getting stuck there! And I sure as hell don't want to get stuck here—it's horrendous!" wailed Cathy.

"Why are you guys still thinking about what was back there? Who cares?" asked Pedro.

"Because it's strange, Pedro! Why would that sign say the next town was there, when nothing was there at all? We're trying to make sense of the fact we had to go there at all!" reasoned Richard.

"But just thinking about it means you're stuck there! Trying to figure it out is just a distraction," said Bill. "In any case, my focus is the Stream, so I don't really care what was there, or what's here."

"Maybe the Stream is here somewhere," said Pedro.

"I sincerely doubt that!" Bill snapped.

Cathy tilted her head, watching him. Something had been bothering her since the start of their journey, and now she felt ready to bring it up.

"Bill, you seem to be constantly in a rush and very impatient. I don't mean to be rude, but I don't think it's exactly helping us along. We're all on this journey together, and we know we have to pass through six towns before we get to the Stream. We're only in the second town, which means we still have four to go."

She paused, looking into his eyes. He was watching her intently, but he seemed to be taking it better than she'd expected. She pushed further, "You know what I think? I think the truth is you're afraid of getting stuck, like Janine, and losing your way."

Bill's eyes narrowed, but he was quiet for a moment before he spoke. "Do I seem afraid?"

Cathy took a deep breath. "Yes. I think you are. Why else would you be in such a hurry to get to the Stream? You're afraid of getting stuck."

"Seriously? You think I'm scared? I'm not scared of anything!"

"Oh, give it up, Bill! You try to be such a tough guy, all arrogant and obnoxious, but I can see right through you! You're obviously just trying to hide your fear!"

She heard Betty gasp and realized what she'd just said. She hadn't meant to be so blunt—she'd only wanted to try to help him. She held her breath, waiting for him to explode, but he didn't.

"Cathy," he instead said quietly. "I think you may be right."

Cathy glanced at the others, who looked just as surprised as she felt. Pedro met her gaze and raised his eyebrows at her.

Bill sighed heavily. "It's just that I know there are going to be temptations along the way, and I don't want to get stuck on the way to paradise."

"That means you're unsure about enjoying where you are, because you're too afraid to get stuck," Richard chimed in. "I think you've carried some ambivalence with you, and you're trying to overcome it by forcing yourself to get somewhere."

"If that's the case," said Cathy slowly, "you won't actually get to the Stream because you can't be ambivalent at the Stream!"

Bill snorted, "And when did you become a know-it-all?"

"Oh, dear," groaned Betty under her breath. "He's back."

"And besides," he continued, gritting his teeth, "I don't think you have to be perfect to get to the Stream."

"We're not talking about perfection, Bill," said Cathy gently. "We're talking about fear. Unless you face your fears, you will spend your life reacting to its effects. You're driven by what you fear, and you seem to see the Stream as something that will save you."

"What's wrong with that? Seth told us that the Stream was *the* ultimate destination, so why can't I see it as my savior?"

"Because," said Richard, "we can only get to the Stream if our inner self is *exactly* the way it would be at the Stream. It's not the Stream that makes us happy—we have to make ourselves happy. Only then will we get to the Stream."

They all went quiet as they contemplated this.

"Alright," said Bill quietly. "I think that's enough."

Cathy knew better than to argue with him. She looked at her companions. "Let's try to get some rest. We've got a big day ahead of us tomorrow. We have to find out what this town is all about!"

Cathy was the third to arrive the next morning—she'd overslept, but Richard and Pedro didn't seem to mind. She'd found them waiting in the lobby—in complete silence. Bill and Betty arrived after her, and they all went into the restaurant for breakfast.

They'd barely given their orders—with no difficulty deciding what they wanted, to Cathy's relief—when Bill began to speak. "I've given a lot of thought to what was said last night. I've come to realize that I wasn't being completely honest about what's going on with me. I see now that my constant pushing—or what Cathy calls my fear—comes from my terror of living a life without meaning, without purpose." He looked at them somberly. "I'm afraid that my time will run out before I have done what I feel called to do."

Cathy felt tears threaten to fill her eyes, but she blinked them back. She guessed Bill would think she was pitying him, and she didn't imagine he would like that one bit. But it wasn't pity; she felt overcome by empathy. How many nights had *she* lain in bed overcome with terror that her entire existence was devoid of meaning?

"So how does hurrying and pushing help you get any closer to meaning and purpose?" she asked him, pouring herself a glass of water from the jug on the table, trying to hide her shaking hands.

He smirked. "It doesn't, really. But doing nothing feels too scary. It feels like death is always chasing me, and if I stop for one second, everything will be over. It's like...." He faltered momentarily. "I feel like my whole life is empty, and I don't want to die feeling this way."

"Lighten up, man!" Pedro burst in, making Cathy jump. "You're way too serious!"

Richard shot him a look. "Pedro, if you don't have anything useful to add, I suggest you keep quiet."

Pedro rolled his eyes.

"So," continued Richard, "are you saying that by constantly moving, and always being in a hurry to do more, you're creating meaning in your life?"

Bill shrugged. "I guess so," he said quietly.

"And has that worked?" asked Cathy.

He let out a long sigh. "Not really. No."

"Bill, this is really powerful stuff," she said gently. "I think everyone here will agree that we all do the same to various extents—we're all running around trying to escape death and trying to find meaning."

"This is starting to feel depressing," Pedro butted in. "What does all this have to do with getting to the Stream, anyway? I think you guys need to chill out."

"You fucking idiot!" Bill roared. He lurched toward Pedro, but Richard jumped up and grabbed him just as his fist swung toward Pedro's face. Richard's intervention was all that prevented Bill from making contact.

"Whoa, dude!" exclaimed a stunned-looking Pedro, standing up and backing away from the table.

Cathy pinched the bridge of her nose. "Let's wrap up here before it gets any worse," she said quietly. "Let's just figure out what Faraway has to offer and what our lesson is here. The sooner we do that, the sooner we can move on and find the Stream."

"Yes," agreed Betty, also looking anxious. "Let's split up and see what this town is all about."

They reconvened in the hotel that evening, meeting in the bar for a pre-dinner drink.

"How was your day, Cathy?" asked Richard, as they sat down.

"You won't believe it! I was doing some window-shopping at a department store nearby, and I got to chatting with the manager. I told him I'd just arrived in town, and he offered me a job recruiting new staff members!" She blushed. "He said I'd be perfect for it with my people skills," she added.

"A similar thing happened to me!" He beamed. "I met a man whose family business is struggling. I've offered to take over and turn things around. I know exactly what needs to be done!"

"Sweet. I got a job as a waiter at the local diner," Pedro told the others.

"Was that the best you could do?" muttered Bill.

Pedro scowled. "What's your problem, man? There's nothing wrong with waiting tables."

"If you say so."

"How about you?" Cathy said, turning to face Bill and Betty.

"I've got a meeting with a local financial company tomorrow to see if they have anything interesting and lucrative to offer me," Bill replied.

"Can't say I did much job-hunting," Betty giggled. "But I did meet a dashingly handsome man, Jeremy, who asked me out on a date tonight!" Her cheeks flushed. "I've spent all day in the beauty salon preparing."

"It shows," said Bill, winking at her and making her giggle like a schoolgirl.

"Betty, that's wonderful!" Cathy gushed, squeezing her hand. "I can't believe how quickly we've settled here! It actually seems like a nice town; I could see myself getting comfortable here. Although I think we'd better find another place to stay," she said, glancing around at the dark, dingy bar.

"I like it here, too, but this heat might become unbearable!" observed Betty, trying to fan herself with a bar napkin.

"I read in the local paper that it hasn't rained in Faraway for decades," Richard told them, prompting Betty to make a face.

"Still, let's stick around here for a while and see what this town is about. We've got jobs and an opportunity to make some cash for our journey," said Bill.

The others nodded in agreement.

"To our new jobs," said Richard, smiling, holding up his drink.

"To our new jobs!" they echoed, clinking glasses.

Cathy found herself easily settling down in Faraway. She grew comfortable, and became so absorbed in her job and new life, that she saw less and less of the others, only meeting up for birthdays and other special occasions as the years flew by.

In the fifth year of her new life in Faraway, Cathy received some bad news: Bill had been in a serious car accident. She met with her travel companions at the hospital, and they greeted each other warmly, if a little nervously. She tried to put on a brave face as they made their way to Bill's room—she hadn't been in a hospital since her own little… accident. It brought back memories she didn't really want to face.

"Oh my goodness, Bill! Are you okay?" said Betty, rushing to his bedside.

"Okay as I can be," he said, managing to smile.

"Wow, man, you look awful," said Pedro.

Cathy rolled her eyes—the young man hadn't changed at all.

"We're just glad to see you're alright!" said Cathy sincerely.

Bill struggled to sit up in his bed. He had stitches on his face, and his arm was in a cast. Betty fussed over him like a mother hen, adjusting his pillow and trying to make him comfortable.

"You know, lying here has got me thinking," he said. "If there's one thing this accident has made me realize, it's that we've completely lost sight of our journey to the Stream. I don't know about you guys, but I've gotten so caught up in my routine here, I forgot about the promise of the Stream."

Cathy's eyes widened. The Stream! When was the last time she had even thought about that?

Richard ran a hand through his hair. "Me too," he admitted. "It seems all I do here is work, sleep, and eat." He frowned, looking at each of them in turn. "But it hasn't been so bad. Has it?"

"Don't you see?" Bill shook his head. "All we've done here is create mundane lives, hoping to find meaning in a town where there *is* no meaning!"

Betty stared down at her hands. "But surely there's got to be meaning here somewhere?" she asked in a small voice.

"That's exactly the point," he told her gently. "There is no meaning, and we're stuck here trying to find it! We're just too afraid to confront the fact that there's nothing here."

"I think you're right," agreed Cathy. "This town has turned us into sleepwalkers! We're like a bunch of zombies who've checked out of life. When was the last time you felt happy?"

"I haven't felt happy since my first date with Jeremy," said Betty sadly. "I hadn't realized how numb I've become. I don't love him anymore, but I just stay with him." She looked on the verge of tears. "All I do here is shop, have my nails done, and lunch with the ladies," she said bitterly.

"Oh, Betty," said Cathy, reaching out to squeeze her hand. "I'm so sorry."

Betty squeezed back and gave her a sad smile.

"I've been working my butt off the last five years, and I've really turned the business around," said Richard. "But I have to admit—I'm bored."

"What does your company do, anyway?" asked Bill.

"We make plastic toothbrushes."

Cathy couldn't help it—she giggled. Richard caught her eye and smiled, and then Bill and Betty were laughing too.

The merriment was brief. The mood dipped again, and they sat in silence for a while, listening to the sound of Bill's heartbeat on the heart monitor.

Bill sighed. "I realize now that all I really want is to get to the Stream. I thought for a long time that I could find paradise here. I thought I didn't need the Stream anymore! But this accident woke me up."

Cathy nodded. "I feel the same." She heard Richard and Betty making noises of assent.

"I like it here," came Pedro's voice, oddly defiant.

As one, they turned to stare at him.

"What?" Betty sounded incredulous.

"Pedro, we're all asleep in this town. We're dying here!" Cathy said, pleading with him to wake up.

He shook his head, backing away from them. "I don't know what you're all on about. My life is fine here. I live alone, and no one bothers me! It's perfect."

Cathy felt her heart sink. "Pedro, if you look at the name of this town, and think about what each of us has experienced here, I think this is the town of *Alienation*."

Richard's eyes lit up. "Yes, I think you're right! We're *far away*—disconnected—here."

"Think about it," Bill said to Pedro. "On the surface, everything we're taught to aspire to is here. We have jobs, money, homes and cars, relationships—everything seems to be in perfect order. We're stuck here because we think we have everything we need, but we feel nothing. No happiness, not even sadness. We're numb here."

"I've got everything I need," said Pedro sullenly. "I've even got a PlayStation *and* a dealer for some pretty great weed."

"Pedro!" Cathy shouted, taking him by the shoulders and shaking him. "Why are you so scared to admit that you don't feel anything?"

"I'm not scared!" He shook her off, scowling.

"Look at you! You're the poster-child for *Alienation*!" Richard frowned at him. "And I'm sick of your dismissive one-liners—everything is not 'fine' and 'cool' all the time!"

Pedro scoffed. "Dude, I don't know what you're talking about. Just chill out!"

"Stop telling us to chill out! You're lying to yourself, Pedro." Richard sounded uncharacteristically furious. "You're a good-for-nothing loser! You sit at home, alone, getting high and playing video games. You hide behind so many walls that I don't think you can see the truth!"

Cathy turned to Pedro. "The way you're reacting, Pedro, reveals where you are. You seem hurt and angry, and it seems like you've adopted a strategy of *pretending* that you're not hurt and pushing people away. Unless you tell yourself the truth about what's happening, you're going to remain in *Alienation*, all alone."

"Shutting down to escape dealing with reality is not going to help," said Bill coldly. "When are you going to realize that crawling into a hole is not going to make things better?"

If their words reached him, he showed no sign. Pedro remained stonily silent.

"Look at you! You're a nothing!" Bill sounded angry as well now. "If you were my son, I would *know* that I'd failed as a parent. I feel sorry for you. You are so alienated from yourself that you don't even know you're alienated!"

"*Alienation* is like a drug, Pedro," Cathy continued, feeling desperate. "It numbs you out, and you get so used to it, you don't even realize what you're doing to yourself."

"Get off my case," Pedro said, not raising his voice or showing any sign of anger. "I'm not doing anything to myself. But I am leaving."

As he reached the door, he turned around and said, "Life is too short. You all need to chill out, or you'll give yourselves heart attacks." With that, he was gone.

Not another one. Cathy looked at the others in disbelief.

"Well, what do we do now?" asked Betty. "I want to get out of here, and I'm ready to leave this minute."

"Me too," Bill agreed. "The doctors say I'll be well enough to leave this evening. Why are we wasting our time dealing with that asshole, anyway?"

"But we can't leave him behind this easily. He has to realize what's going on here! This town is the pits—how can we leave him here?" Cathy felt like bursting into tears.

"Cathy," Richard said gently. "If he doesn't wake up now, it might take a more jarring experience to do it, like Bill had. But we aren't responsible for making that happen. The four of us are ready to move on, and we're learning the lessons for ourselves. We can't force him."

Cathy sighed. "You're right. I know you are. I just can't believe we're losing another one."

Betty patted her shoulder. "I know, Cathy. But we've settled here, in more ways than one. And it's definitely time to get going."

They decided to go home to pack their things, and meet in the town square the next morning. Cathy left a message on Pedro's answering machine, letting him know that they were leaving, and he was free to join them if he wanted to.

Cathy was in the middle of packing later that evening when Richard called.

"Hey, I need a couple more days to tie up some things. Can we leave next week?"

"No, Richard. We've made a plan to leave tomorrow and that's that." She was surprised by her own assertive tone, and softened her voice. "We've been stuck here too long, Richard. We have to leave before everyone changes their minds!"

"Come on, Cathy! Please?"

"Richard, we both know you're only doing this because you're too afraid to leave Faraway. Trust me, I am too. I know we have no idea what the next town is going to be like, but we have to leave here if we're to get to the Stream."

There was silence for a moment.

Cathy sighed. "Richard, I would truly hate to continue this journey without you, but I'm not going to push you. We decided to let Pedro stay, and we will do the same with you. But please reconsider," she pleaded.

"Okay, Cathy," he said, his voice small, before hanging up.

Early the next morning, Cathy, Bill, and Betty met in the town square with their bags packed, ready to leave. Cathy looked around desperately for any sign of Pedro or Richard. At the last moment, a taxi pulled up; after what seemed like ages, the door opened, and Richard's smiling face greeted her.

"Ok, gang! Let's get this show on the road!" he said brightly.

Betty looked around the town, sighing. "I'm really sorry that Pedro decided to stay," she said. "But I can't say I'm surprised."

"Yeah," replied Bill. "If he doesn't want to deal with his crap, then screw him."

The travelers began their trek out of Faraway, and Cathy felt sad about the people and the things they were leaving behind. Even though their life in *Alienation* was rooted in nothingness, she'd become used to it: there were many things she was going to miss. Although she didn't want to say so out loud, she knew she would miss Pedro, even though she couldn't pinpoint exactly why.

"I hope it's cooler in the next town," said Richard.

"Me too! I never thought I'd say this, but I miss the rain!" Cathy replied. She remembered Seth's apparently irrational question about whether she preferred warm weather or cool, and smiled to herself. What a journey this was turning out to be.

CHAPTER 6

A few hours after leaving *Faraway*, the intense heat finally subsided, and the travelers were treated to a gentle, cool breeze. It was so deliciously refreshing that when they stopped to take a break in the shade of a beautiful old oak tree, Bill and Betty decided to take a nap.

They looked so peaceful as they slept that Cathy felt envious. As lovely as the breeze felt on her skin, as comfortable as it was in the shade, she just couldn't relax. She leaned toward Richard and whispered, "I can't help feeling sad for the five years we lost in Faraway."

Richard sighed, nodding his head. "I know what you mean. There's so much we could have been doing on our journey, but we chose to spend it in mediocrity. It's pretty depressing." He reached over and patted her hand. "I know how you must be feeling, but it's best not to dwell on it, Cathy."

As if it's so simple! Cathy leaned back against the grass, watching the clouds drifting through the sky. *I can't just stop feeling my feelings!* she protested silently.

After maybe half an hour, Bill woke up, looking refreshed and energized. "Time to get moving!" he said, stretching like a cat.

He turned to her and grinned, and she found herself smiling back. He was so different when he was in a good mood—almost charming.

They woke Betty and started walking again, faster this time: dusk was approaching, and they were keen to get settled before nightfall.

Cathy was lagging behind, still unable to shake her melancholy, when she heard Betty call: "Come on, you lot! Keep up!"

She looked up to find Betty beckoning to her and Richard. "I've spotted the next town!" she told them. "Look!"

As they drew nearer, they found Bill contemplating the large sign outside the town. "*Welcome to Loss*," he read. He raised an eyebrow at them. "That doesn't sound like fun."

"Oh no, that doesn't sound fun at all!" Cathy wailed. "Maybe this isn't the next town! I'm sure I saw another path back there!" she babbled, not sure if they'd believe her.

"Cathy," Richard said, taking her gently by the shoulders. "This is the only town for miles, and you know it. If we don't go through Loss, we'll never get to the Stream."

She sighed heavily. "I know." She shrugged. "Let's see what it's about, then," she said, and they continued along the path to *Loss*.

As they got closer, Bill looked over his shoulder at them, frowning. "What's with all the funeral parlors?"

"It's pretty creepy," Cathy agreed. She'd been wondering the same thing; she didn't think she'd ever seen so many in one place before.

"Let's just find a hotel for the night and try to get out of here as soon as possible," Richard whispered.

"I'm exhausted!" Betty moaned. "How much further can it be?"

Bill smirked, "Unless you want to hitch a ride with a hearse, I suggest you keep walking."

Betty rolled her eyes and answered with a sigh, "I'm too tired to argue with you, Bill."

When they reached the center of town, Betty pointed excitedly. "Look, there's a hotel!" she said.

But as they approached, they saw a large *To Let* sign in the window.

"Oh, no. It's closed down," said Richard.

Cathy looked around anxiously. "So is that one on the other side of the square," she said, pointing to the boarded-up windows.

"This is ridiculous!" Bill growled. "Why are all these hotels closed? What kind of business practice is this?"

Betty stopped a passer-by and asked where they could find a hotel that was open for business.

"Oh, yeah, these hotels open and close all the time," he said nonchalantly. He directed them to a hotel called the Mayfair, which was not only open, but also five stars, to Cathy's overwhelming delight.

After checking into their rooms, they met in the restaurant for lunch. Cathy felt like she could eat a horse, but after waiting about fifteen minutes, they hadn't been approached by any servers.

"What the hell is going on here?" shouted Bill, banging his fist into the table.

"Ssh!" hissed Cathy. "Lower your voice, Bill. I'm sure someone will serve us eventually."

About five minutes later, a waiter appeared and apologized for the poor service.

"We're short-staffed," he explained. "Three people lost their jobs this week, so there are only two of us working lunch today. I'm so sorry, but you'll have to excuse us if the service is a bit slow!"

Once he'd taken their orders and left the table, Cathy looked at the others. "I wonder why so many people lost their jobs?"

"I'm about to lose my temper," Bill muttered.

Betty rolled her eyes. "I think that ship has sailed," she said under her breath.

The food finally arrived—to Cathy's great relief—and she felt much better for being able to fill her stomach.

After they'd eaten, they decided to split up and explore the town separately. They parted ways and agreed to meet back at the hotel that evening.

Betty walked along the main street, looking at the window displays of the different shops. She hadn't made it far when she was stopped by a friendly young man holding a clipboard.

"Hi there!" he said brightly. "How would you like to feed a hungry child?"

Betty noticed the pamphlets he was holding and a large bucket of change at his side.

"*Children without Parents* is a great cause," he continued. "We take care of orphaned children until we find suitable homes for them. We're actually having a festival in the town square tomorrow to raise money. If you have time, you should come along!"

"Wow, it looks like you do some great work," Betty replied, taking a pamphlet. "I'll certainly be there!"

She dropped a $100 bill in the bucket and went on her way, a broad smile on her face.

Cathy spent the afternoon exploring the area around the hotel. Apart from the numerous funeral parlors, she also noticed an abundance of retirement villages.

Everyone must be really old in this town, she thought to herself.

She stopped at a café to have a cup of coffee and sat down next to a young woman who was talking on her cell phone.

"Now that the divorce is finalized, Anthony's left town," Cathy heard the woman say. "He doesn't care about his son! He's just left us to fend for ourselves!"

Cathy sipped her coffee, trying her best not to eavesdrop.

"Stop telling me it's going to be OK! You're not the one with cancer!" the woman shouted into her phone. She broke down in tears, "A year ago, the doctor told me I was in remission. Now I'm back on the chemo, and it's not doing anything!"

Cathy gasped. She couldn't believe what she was hearing.

"But you're not here," the woman continued quietly. "No one is here. Anthony was all I had left, and he's gone."

The woman's sobbing intensified, and Cathy moved her attention elsewhere, wanting to give her some privacy. She focused on drinking her coffee, trying to convince herself not to get involved, but this woman was a mother, like her, and she was dying.

Cathy leaned over to her. "I'm sorry, miss? I don't mean to pry, but I couldn't help overhearing your conversation. I know this is going to sound weird coming from a complete stranger, but is there anything I could do?"

The woman looked at her with red-rimmed eyes, "I don't think so."

Cathy felt her heart melt. "I'm Cathy," she said, and then added, "And I'm a mother too."

The woman eyed her wearily but eventually said, "I'm Leanne."

"Leanne, here's my number," Cathy said, scribbling it on a piece of paper. "If you need anything, please call me. I know how useful an extra set of hands can be!"

"Thank you," she said, wiping her eyes. "That's really kind of you. Things have been tough lately." She paused to drain her cup of the last sip of coffee. "I've got to run, otherwise I'll be late fetching my son from school."

"Please call me." Cathy squeezed Leanne's arm as she stood, and looked into her eyes sincerely, "I mean it."

That evening, the travelers met in the restaurant for dinner. The same waiter who had served them at lunch came to take their orders.

"This is my last shift," he told them sadly. "The reason my colleagues lost their jobs is because the hotel is closing down at the end of the week."

"What the hell goes on in this place?" Bill mumbled in irritation.

As the waiter walked away, a man approached the table and introduced himself as the owner. They asked if it was true that he was closing down the hotel.

"I'm afraid it is," he said, clearly down heartened. "Things haven't turned out the way I had hoped."

"How awful!" sympathized Cathy.

"Yeah," he sighed. "I bought this place hoping my son would join me and take over the business, but he moved away to go to college. I rarely hear from him anymore... and, truth be told, I don't even think he's coming back. I thought we'd be the next Hiltons!" He laughed, but there was no real humor behind it. "Anyway, I think it'll be best to close it down and move into a retirement village."

"But you aren't nearly old enough!" Cathy blurted out, before realizing how rude that sounded.

He shrugged, "That's what everyone does here when they have nowhere else to go," he replied. "My wife died years ago. My son was all I had left."

The travelers were silent for a moment as the owner drifted away from the table.

"I think I'm starting to understand why this town is called *Loss*," said Cathy quietly.

Richard's phone rang, and he excused himself from the table to take the call.

A Journey to the Stream

"Listen to this," said Betty brightly, setting a pamphlet down on the table. "There's a wonderful charity in this town called Children without Parents. They're having a festival tomorrow in the town square, and I think we should all go and support them! It's a great cause."

"That sounds interesting! We should definitely do that," agreed Cathy. She was keen for a distraction to take her mind off Leanne's troubles, which kept resurfacing in her thoughts. She turned to Bill, "What did you get up to today?"

"No charities for me," he admitted. "But I have found a lucrative business opportunity."

"Of course you have!" Betty and Cathy chanted in unison.

"Scoff all you want!" said Bill, mock-scowling. "You can take the businessman out of the boardroom, but you can't take the boardroom out of the businessman!"

"What business is it?" Cathy asked, as their food arrived. "I was starting to think this town was in a recession!"

"No, they are definitely not in a recession. It's just that not all businesses end up a success. Lots of companies close down—just look at these hotels—so I thought I'd do some business consulting while I'm here, dealing with company takeovers and breaking up businesses that are struggling, selling off assets and so on. It's a no-brainer!"

He looked happy—like a little kid with a new toy. Cathy caught Betty's eye, and they shared a smile.

They were finishing their meal when Richard rejoined the table. His face was ashen.

"I have a problem," he said quietly as he sat down.

"What's the matter?" asked Cathy, her voice full of concern.

"I've just had a call from Faraway. The business manager I left in charge of my finances has run away. I've lost… everything. All my money is gone!"

"My goodness, Richard, that's terrible!" said Betty.

"I'm really sorry, but I have to go back to Faraway to sort this out. I've got to find that bastard."

Cathy gasped. "No, Richard, you can't!" she wailed.

"Of course I can! How can I go on with absolutely no money?"

"I can't even imagine what that must be like," said Bill quietly.

"I see Bill's finally found his empathy," snickered Betty. "For money, of course!"

"Richard," said Cathy turning to face him. "You can't go back there! Think about the Stream. All you need will be at the Stream!"

"Don't give me that," snapped Richard. "I need my money! I can't go on with nothing! I just can't."

Cathy was taken aback. She had never seen him so angry.

"Cathy's right, Richard," said Bill. "You've got a choice here: either your money or the Stream."

"Why can't I have both? I'll catch up with you guys when I'm done."

"But hold on a moment," said Cathy as realization dawned. "This town is *Loss*! Don't you realize that you'll lose your money all over again when you come back here?"

He shrugged. "That might be true. All I know is that it feels insane not to take care of my financial responsibility in the hope that all that I need is waiting for me at some Stream. A man's got to eat!"

"You and I both know that you can make enough money to feed yourself, no matter where you are! It's not about that at all!" Cathy found she was getting angry herself.

He sighed. "Fine, so I want to live a certain way. I like my comforts. What's wrong with that?"

"What's wrong with it is it makes you lose sight of the Stream! What's more important than that?"

"Look, Cathy. I'm sorry, but I really don't want to start over. I invested all my money in Faraway, and some punk has run off with the profits. I'm going back there to fix this. I don't believe I have to give up my money to get to the Stream."

Cathy struggled to contain the lump forming in her throat. She couldn't believe she was losing someone she had connected with so well on this journey.

"I promise you," Richard said, taking her hands, "I will not lose sight of the Stream. And I *will* catch up to you."

With that, he bid farewell to his fellow travelers and was gone.

"Well, I don't know about you two, but I'm keen to stick around for a while," said Betty. "If we do, though, we'll have to arrange new accommodation." She looked around at the hotel that was soon to close down.

"Sounds good to me," agreed Bill.

Cathy smiled and nodded, but was inwardly too shocked at what had happened. She declined post-dinner drinks and retired to her room in a daze, too exhausted and sad to do anything else but sleep.

The following morning, Cathy found Bill waiting for her in the lobby. The hotel was abuzz with liquidators and workers, who were already moving out the furniture and starting to dismantle the fittings.

"Where's Betty?" Bill asked.

"She knocked on my door first thing this morning to say that we shouldn't wait for her. She went to the square to help Children without Parents. Have you heard from Richard?"

Cathy's phone rang before Bill could respond. She apologized, but he waved her off, watching the workers interestedly, and she answered the call.

"Cathy?" The voice on the other end of the line sounded tentative, "It's Leanne."

"Leanne, hi!"

"I'm sorry. I wouldn't have called if it wasn't urgent," Leanne said, sounding frazzled. "The hospital just called to say my latest dose of medicine is ready for collection, but I just can't make it there today. Would it be a huge bother if I asked you to do it?"

"Not at all!" said Cathy kindly. "I meant it when I said I would help you!"

Leanne gave Cathy the details, and they arranged to meet at her house later.

As Cathy ended the call, Bill looked at her curiously. "When did you have time to make friends?"

"It's the most heartbreaking story," said Cathy. "This woman's been left all alone to raise her young son. To make matters worse, she's got cancer… and by the sound of things, she doesn't have long to live. I told her I'd help her out."

"Hmm," said Bill, nodding.

Cathy didn't think he'd heard a word she'd said. He was waving to one of the men talking to the owner of the hotel. "A business associate," he said by way of explanation when he saw her looking curious.

Cathy sighed inwardly, "Let's go find Betty and see what's keeping her so busy," she said.

When they reached the town square, they found Betty in full action, seated behind a table and selling cakes.

"Wow, she looks quite involved already," Cathy whispered.

Eventually, Betty came over to them, wiping her hands on her apron.

"We're so busy! This has been a *huge* success! It's not even lunchtime and we've already raised enough money to house 30 orphans for a month!" she said excitedly.

"*We?*" said Bill, raising an eyebrow.

She scowled at him. "These people need me!" she said. "Not just my money, but my time. These poor children have nothing else. The money we raise can really help them!"

"I think it's great," said Cathy, smiling at her.

"I better get back to work!" She giggled. "In 50 years, I never thought I'd say that!" She left them and returned to her spot behind the table.

"For a woman who hasn't worked a day in her life, she's doing a good job," said Cathy. "I think it's admirable that she wants to give back."

"Well, I better get to work, too," said Bill, looking at his watch. "Companies aren't going to sell off themselves!"

"And I better get Leanne's medication," said Cathy. "See you later!"

When Cathy arrived at Leanne's house, the piles of dirty dishes in the kitchen and the unmade beds made her heart sink.

She made tea as Leanne told her about the divorce and the day she learned she had cancer.

"The first thing I thought was, 'Who is going to take care of Jackson?'" she said, looking sadly at her young boy who was playing with his toy train on the carpet.

Cathy's eyes welled up. She wished she could do something to give the woman some comfort.

As Leanne helped her son with his homework, Cathy cleaned the kitchen, made the beds, and threw a load of laundry into the washing machine. She cooked dinner for them, and as she was about to leave, Leanne asked her to join them.

Cathy shook her head, "I don't want to intrude."

"Don't be silly!" Leanne replied. "After everything you've done for us today, the least I can do is offer you a meal, even if you're the one who cooked it!"

For the next few weeks after that, Cathy found herself spending every day with Leanne and Jackson, helping with chores around the house and running errands. She could think of nothing but the mother who didn't have much time left with her child.

Four weeks later, Cathy was out buying some groceries when she bumped into Bill outside the supermarket.

"Bill!" She had never felt so relieved to see a friendly face, even if it was Bill's. Her throat tightened up. "I have terrible news," she told him. "Leanne's dead."

"What? I didn't realize it was that close to the end!"

"She's gone, Bill!" Cathy wailed. "I don't know what to do. I can't leave her little boy alone. He's got no one!"

"Cathy, we can't stay here forever," he reminded her gently.

"I know but I can't leave. Jackson needs me now that his mother is dead. I can't just leave him!"

Bill looked thoughtful. "Cathy, we've been in Loss for over a month. I've been thinking about it, and I really think it may be time to continue on our journey to the Stream."

"The Stream can wait!" she nearly snarled back. "How can I let this child lose the only person in his life?"

She started to cry, unable to keep the tears in anymore. Bill awkwardly tried to pat her on the shoulder, but she pulled away.

"Alright, take it easy," he said, softly. "Let's meet for breakfast tomorrow at the Bluebird Café. I'll call Betty too. It'll be good to catch up."

Cathy nodded as she scrounged in her bag for a tissue.

"See you tomorrow," he said warmly.

Bill was the first to arrive at the café and got them a table outside. He watched the people of Loss walking by as he waited for Cathy and Betty. He'd been noticing more and more lately how sad everyone looked.

He was ordering a glass of orange juice when Cathy and Betty arrived. They both seemed to be flustered.

"What's with you two this morning? What's the rush?"

"Oh, I can't stay long. I told Jackson's babysitter I'd be back in an hour," Cathy replied, looking agitated.

"And I've got a meeting at Children without Parents at 11:00, so I can't stay long either," Betty told him.

Bill sighed, "I can't believe I've been stuck alone with you two!" he grumbled.

"Bill!" Cathy exclaimed. "I've been through so much these past few weeks; I really don't need this right now!"

Betty shook her head at him angrily as well, "Why are you picking on us, anyway?"

Bill sighed, "Alright, alright. I'm not picking on anyone. It's just that I think we've lost sight of the Stream, and it may be a good time to carry on with our journey."

"I'm not so sure about that," said Betty warily. "Children without Parents have just appointed me Chairperson. I'm making a huge contribution to this charity."

"Wow, Betty, that's incredible!" Cathy's eyes lit up.

"That's very philanthropic of you," said Bill mildly. "But don't you remember the *promise* of the Stream?"

Betty raised an eyebrow at him. "Yes, Bill, I remember the promise of the Stream," she said, speaking slowly, as if he were a child. "But that's all it is: a promise! How can I believe in something I've never seen?"

He was aghast. "Betty, can't you see that…."

"My life has meaning here!" she interrupted. "For the first time in… I don't know, forever? I actually feel *connected*. These people *need* me. I can't just up and go!"

Bill frowned. "Betty, can't you see that in this town there will always be someone who 'needs' you? What you two are doing is making excuses because you're too afraid to let go."

"I don't know what you mean," said Betty stiffly. "What I have here is more than I've ever had before. Sure, my whole life I've had everything anyone could ever want *materially*. But I've been missing a deeper connection to a sense of purpose. And I've found it here." She lifted her chin, looking determined. "My purpose is to help these children. And I don't want to risk not having a purpose again!"

"I agree with her," said Cathy, looking angry. "At least what we're doing here is meaningful. Unlike you, Bill, making money off of people losing their businesses!"

He raised his eyebrows at her. "Judge all you want, sweetheart. At least I'm not caught up in some twisted sense of *purpose*."

"You're so full of crap," Betty spat, her cheeks flushing.

He shook his head slowly. "Do you know what I think?" he said. "This must be the town of *Abandonment*. It's the home of suffering. Everything that happens here is experienced as loss." He looked them both in the eye. "I think you have to be able to see that before you can move on."

Cathy's eyes widened, and Bill felt like he was getting through to her, at least.

"No matter what the circumstances, the best place to help anyone is from the Stream," he said quietly. "The faster you get there, the more you'll be able to help others."

"I think Bill may be right," said Cathy slowly. "I've been taking care of a little boy who lost his mother. I'm all he has right now, and leaving him may be the most painful thing I'll ever have to do, but I think I might have to. For me *and* for my journey to the Stream." She wiped a tear from her cheek. "Call me selfish!" she muttered, as if answering someone. "But I know that there are organizations, like Betty's, that can look after Jackson." She turned to Betty, who just shook her head.

"I'm sorry," Betty said, sadly but firmly. "You'll have to continue without me. Leaving here means leaving *everything* behind for an idea, for a promise we got from some guy none of us had ever met before. I just can't do it. I'm not leaving."

"Please, Betty," Cathy pleaded. "You have to trust that the Stream is better than all of this!"

"I don't," Betty said simply. "I've never believed that life was a fairytale, and

I'm certainly not about to start now. I *can't* have faith that things will be better if I can't see what's on the other end." She met Bill's gaze, her eyes resolute. "I've found meaning in my life for the first time. I am *not* about to give that up."

"Come on, Betty!" Cathy wailed. "We *all* have something we need, and if we're getting even a little bit of it from something, we cling to it. And I think that's what you're doing here!" She paused. "Do you think leaving an orphaned child is easy for me?" she asked in a quieter tone. "You should be able to let go of rescuing people. I think you're using it as an excuse. I don't know what's out there, either, but that doesn't mean I've given up faith."

Betty shook her head again. "*You* can live your life in faith and hope and trust that whatever is out there is better than what is here. But I *can't*."

Bill looked at Cathy and saw the sadness in her eyes. Neither of them would be able to get through to Betty. *Abandonment* would be hard to shake, and Betty would have to be able to abandon this town on her own.

Without staying another night, Bill and Cathy walked away from the town of *Loss*. As they walked past the funeral parlors and retirement villages, Cathy turned to Bill. She knew that they didn't quite see eye to eye about everything, but he was all she had left as they continued their journey.

"I'm scared," she admitted. "Letting go and moving on from this town means stepping into a great unknown. I can't know the unknowable, and that frightens me."

"I know what you mean," he replied quietly.

They kept walking until Bill stopped and turned to her. "How about this: let's say we meet the next town with *excitement* instead of fear. We know that we're halfway to the Stream, and whatever comes next is one step closer."

Cathy nodded. "Sounds like a plan," she replied.

She found she felt a tiny bit better as they walked. Whatever was next, she knew that the only thing that really mattered was that she was out of *Abandonment*.

CHAPTER 7

Bill felt like he was at his wits end. They'd been walking for miles, but Cathy hadn't cheered up much at all since they left *Loss*: she talked about being excited for the next town, but kept falling back into crying and sniffling the whole way. He'd been trying to remain supportive, but he was finding it increasingly difficult.

"Cathy, I know it's hard, but you need to look forward, not backward! Think of the Stream! Everything you want will be there! Doesn't that excite you?"

"I guess," she said, shrugging her shoulders.

Bill was biting back a snarky response for the hundredth time when Cathy burst out, "Do you smell that?"

He turned to face the breeze and inhaled deeply. *That smells like...* "Is that the sea?" he asked in disbelief.

"I think it is. Look!" Cathy pointed excitedly at what turned out to be a long stretch of sandy white beach.

They ran toward it as fast as they could, whooping and cheering, and planted their feet in the smooth, soft sand. Looked out towards the endless expanse of sea that lay before them, Bill felt his face split into a grin. This was certainly a very pleasant surprise.

"This is so beautiful!" Cathy exclaimed in awe.

"It's absolutely spectacular!" he agreed. "Whatever this is, I like it already!"

"Oh my goodness!" Cathy exclaimed as she looked around. Behind them was a metropolis, a vast array of futuristic skyscrapers backed right up to the beach. The light from the buildings was dazzling.

"Where do we even start?" murmured Cathy, sounding amazed.

Bill grinned at her. "Let's start by finding a hotel. I could use a shower. And then I'm going to spend all afternoon on this amazing beach!"

They spotted an Information Office and decided to go in and ask for advice. There was an attractive woman standing behind the counter, and she greeted them with a dazzling smile as they approached.

"We're looking for a hotel. And it's got to be near the beach!" Bill told her.

"Well, sir, this beach stretches for miles and hotels run all along it, so you'll have to give me a few more specifics."

Bill looked at Cathy as though he had just won the jackpot.

"Okay, then. Let's say we're looking for rooms around $100 a night."

"That's better! Here's a map," she said, fetching one from under the counter and spreading it out. "There are about 500 of them within 5 miles of here...."

"What? Are you serious?" Cathy couldn't believe what she was hearing.

"I'll show you which hotels I recommend. They're all five star," she announced with a note of pride. After highlighting her choice of hotels, she handed the travelers the map.

"But you've circled 250 hotels," said Cathy, feeling lost just looking at the map. "That's half of all the hotels in the area!"

She smiled. "Yes, madam, those are my recommendations."

"How are we ever going to choose just one? Could you maybe narrow it down to two or three?"

The lady just shrugged.

As they were leaving, Bill turned to her and asked, "What's the name of this town, anyway?"

"Oh, it's the town of *Plenty*, sir."

Bill raised his eyebrows. "Figures," he said, smirking.

Bill fumbled with the map, trying to decide which direction they should take. "This is madness! I wish we could stay at all of these hotels! How are we going to pick one?"

"Don't look at me!" Cathy replied. "250 hotels, all of them five star, with rooms for $100 a night, on the beach within 5 miles of here! What could be better?"

He sighed and crumpled the map up. "Okay. Let's just walk and see which one we come across first."

As they walked, they noticed that the town was laid out on a grid and each street looked exactly like the next. There were people everywhere, all carrying dozens of shopping bags, and only the finest, most expensive cars lined the sidewalks. They walked along the beachfront promenade until Cathy spotted one of the recommended hotels.

"That one looks good!" she said, pointing. The enormous complex looked like an entire village.

"Yeah, but look at that one," Bill responded, pointing to a skyscraper in the opposite direction. "The gym overlooks the sea with floor-to-ceiling windows—look at all those gorgeous women working out!"

Cathy shook her head and sighed. "Why don't we stay at the complex for one night, and we can move to the skyscraper with the gym tomorrow?"

"Great plan! Then we'll get the chance to sample more than one of these incredible hotels!"

They approached the entrance of the complex—aptly named Perfect Beach Resort—and were promptly directed onto a golf cart. They were then driven up the sweeping driveway, which was lined with palm trees and large manicured lawns.

Cathy looked at Bill in disbelief. "What is this place?" she mouthed.

"Heaven," he replied simply.

When they reached the reception area. Bill asked for two rooms for the night.

"No problem," said the receptionist, clicking away at her keyboard. "We have 48 rooms available in your price range. Which would you like?"

"Aren't they all the same?" Cathy asked, puzzled.

"No, madam. We have bungalows closest to the sea, which all come with your own private butler and chef. The adjacent ones are closest to the restaurant, and all food and drinks are included in the price. The bungalows closest to reception come with free...."

"Okay, okay!" Bill cut her off. "How about we take two rooms with the butler and chef?" He looked at Cathy questioningly, and she nodded excitedly in agreement.

"Very good, sir."

Before they could blink, they were handed two key cards and a welcome brochure, and a porter was summoned to take their luggage to their rooms. A waiter appeared as if from nowhere and offered them a tray of champagne glasses.

"These are Cristal," he said pointing to one side of the tray, "and these are Bollinger. If you would prefer, I also have Moët & Chandon, Taittinger, Laurent-Perrier...."

"We'll just have these, thank you," Cathy interrupted, lifting two glasses of Cristal off the tray.

Bill looked at her in surprise.

"What, you think I don't know my Cristal from my Taittinger? Believe it or not, I do know about the finer things in life," she said cheekily. She was already feeling at ease and relaxed in this town.

Bill smiled. "I could get used to this!" he said. He took a big gulp of champagne, and they made their way to their rooms.

After taking a quick nap and freshening up, Cathy made her way down to the beach. Bill was already there, sprawled on a sun lounger. A gorgeous waitress was serving him a cocktail, and as Cathy approached, she noticed Bill whispering seductively in the woman's ear.

"Bill! Try not to get too comfortable here! Remember, we're only stopping in."

He mock scowled at her. "Oh, Cathy, always the spoilsport! Here, have a cocktail!"

Cathy looked at the array of cocktails on the table between them. *Like a rainbow,* she mused.

She chose the bluest cocktail from among them and took a sip. Then she put it down and tried another color. And then another. And another.

"What are you doing?" Bill asked quizzically.

"I want to sample them all," Cathy giggled.

As she sipped, Cathy watched the waves crashing against the beach. She loved the sea and felt grateful to be here after the harrowing experience she'd had in *Abandonment*.

After a while, she turned to Bill. "So, what do you think this place is all about?"

"That's not hard—Plenty has got to be about choices! There's so much on offer! Unlike *Ambivalence*, though, we can make decisions here. Plus, I think this place is definitely about indulgence," he said, eyeing the waitress, who had returned with more drinks.

Cathy pondered this for a moment. "You know, I think you may be right. *Abandonment* was about loss, and if you think about it, whenever you choose something, you lose whatever it is you *don't* choose. Once you move beyond that loss, you can just make decisions based on what's best, rather than on whether you'll experience a sense of loss."

Bill nodded. "I'm always right, sweetheart," he said, winking.

They stayed there for the rest of the afternoon, enjoying the beach, the sunshine, and the cocktails.

As the sun began to set, Cathy started to get ready to go back to the hotel.

"Bill, this place is fabulous and it's *just* what I need after *Loss*, but we mustn't forget the Stream and how close it is to us now! How about we stay here for the weekend, enjoy what's here, and leave on Monday?"

"Another great plan!" He smiled broadly, "I think we've already aced this town!"

Monday morning found Cathy enjoying a leisurely breakfast on the verandah of her bungalow. She had enjoyed the services of her butler and chef and would definitely miss them. While she had chosen to stay at Perfect Beach, Bill had moved across to the skyscraper hotel across the road. She hadn't seen him all weekend.

She got ready and walked across to his hotel, aptly named *As High as It Gets*, and went to reception to find his room. The receptionist giggled at the sound of his name and directed Cathy to the 50_{th} floor. Cathy gave her a puzzled look and made her way up to his room. She knocked on the door once, then twice. Just as she was beginning to worry, Bill opened the door, wearing nothing but a towel.

"Oh! Bill, I'm so sorry!" said Cathy, blushing, trying to avert her eyes.

"No worries," he said, leaning against the doorframe. He was looking at Cathy expectantly.

"It's just that it's Monday, and remember we said that we would…."

"Be right there!" Bill shouted over his shoulder.

"Oh! I didn't realize you had company! I'll come back later!" Cathy said, turning and backing away from Bill's room, uncharacteristically flustered at the thought of Bill with a "special" guest.

"Meet me at the pool bar in 30 minutes," he called after her.

Cathy had regained her composure by the time Bill arrived at the bar—15 minutes late. He ordered a beer from the barman, and almost instantly, the barman put two beers in front of him.

"It's always two-for-one here," he explained.

"Yes lovely, now you want to tell me about your weekend, Casanova?" Cathy teased.

Bill stifled a laugh. "Cathy, you won't believe it. On Saturday, I went to the hotel gym, and while I was working out, all these beautiful women just started smiling at me! It was amazing!"

"Sure sounds amazing," said Cathy sarcastically.

"I couldn't believe how easy it all was! The only problem was I couldn't decide on just one—so I had them all!"

Cathy rolled her eyes. As much as part of her wanted to scold him, she badly wanted to tell him about her weekend: she was so excited that she couldn't hold it in any longer.

"Good. I don't need the details! While I was exploring Plenty, I met the friendliest guy at a book shop in town. He invited me to a café where he was meeting with friends. They were the most interesting people I've ever met—authors, poets, artists, actors—so many creative types! We talked and laughed all afternoon, and I fit right in immediately. I love this place!"

They sipped their drinks together until Bill eventually voiced what Cathy had been thinking. "I think this might be the Stream," he said quietly.

"But it can't be! It's only the fourth town. Remember, we have to go through six towns to get to the Stream." She rubbed her forehead. "But it does seem like the Stream... I just don't get it."

"Stop over-thinking this, Cathy. Just let it be!"

"I can't! Everything I've ever wanted seems available here... I can't imagine it getting any better than this!"

"Alright, let's test it. What is something you've always wanted?"

She shifted in her chair. "Well, the truth is, I love painting. I've always wanted to teach art. Spending time with all those artists over the weekend made me realize it all over again!"

"That's perfect! Why don't you post an advert saying that you're looking for art students and see what happens?"

Cathy's eyes widened. "That's a great idea! I'm going to do it today!" She frowned. "But that means we'll have to spend a few more days here."

Bill smiled broadly, "Fine with me!"

Cathy chuckled at this mischievous side of Bill and picked up a newspaper from the end of the bar, looking for the number to call.

"I'm excited to see the response," she told Bill. "If this really is the Stream, all my dreams will come true here!"

"Mine already have," said Bill, winking at the cocktail waitress.

Two days later, the travelers met again for breakfast, this time on the patio of the restaurant in Cathy's hotel.

Bill had hardly sat down when Cathy turned to him, eyes wide. "Bill, I've had almost 2000 responses to my ad!"

He raised his eyebrows. "That's amazing! But why do you look so confused?"

"I'm completely overwhelmed!" she said, almost sobbing. "I have no way of processing all of this! I thought one or two would be great, but 2000? What on earth am I going to do?"

"Okay, Cathy, calm down. I think this town may be more complicated than we thought."

She hardly heard him. "This is too much!" She wailed. "Too much!"

"Cathy," he said, gently squeezing her shoulder. "Why don't you start by choosing just a few students to reply to?"

She stared at him. "You're right," she said, feeling herself start to relax. "I didn't think of that. I'll choose a few people who look promising and take it from there." She smiled. "Thank you, Bill."

"No problem, Cath," he murmured, making Cathy sigh. His attention was already on the new waitresses who'd come in.

A week later, Cathy held her first art class on the beach. She met with twelve students, and they spent two hours painting various beach scenes under Cathy's tutelage.

She enjoyed teaching the class just as much as she'd always imagined she would, and she continued to teach for the next couple of weeks. Her classes slowly grew as she took on more and more students, and she took them all over town, sketching and painting various scenes.

The more popular Cathy became, the more she started to charge for her classes. After a few months, she was making more money than she'd thought was possible for an art teacher. It felt good to be earning so much, and she could see the appreciation her students had for her—it brought Cathy great joy to watch their talent grow and develop. At the same time, though, she found herself feeling more and more unsettled. She did her best to ignore the uneasy feeling that was creeping up inside her, but it made no difference. The feelings just grew stronger.

Finally, she'd had enough, and she decided that she needed to talk to Bill. She called him, and they arranged to meet at a restaurant in town. She was waiting for him at an outside table when she heard a ferocious roar. When she turned, slightly startled, she saw a shiny, new Ferrari driving up—with Bill in the driver's seat.

"Not bad," she said, nodding at the car as he sat down.

He winked at her and hailed the waiter to order a bottle of champagne. It arrived within moments, perfectly chilled, and he poured them each a glass.

"A toast!" he said with a smile. "To us, and to *Plenty!*"

Cathy found she couldn't return his smile. "I'm sorry, Bill... I think something really weird is going on here."

His smile faded, "Weird how?"

"Well, it's just... You know I've been teaching classes for a while now, and I'm making some pretty good money. But the truth is, I just don't think I'm that into it anymore."

He tilted his head. "I don't think I understand," he said slowly. "Wasn't this a dream of yours?"

"It is." She paused to think, and then tried to put the vague feeling into words, "It's like… I enjoy parts of it, but not all of it. I don't know. It's difficult to explain, but I just don't think I want to be doing it anymore."

"But I thought this was what you'd always wanted! You'll have to explain a bit more for me to understand what's going on here."

"Okay, yes, well, you're right. This *is* what I've always wanted. But the crazy thing is, now that I've got it—in bucket loads—I just don't know if I'm that excited about it anymore!"

"What on earth are you talking about?" he asked, looking at her like she'd grown a second head.

She chewed her lip. "Well, I've got all these students, but I just don't feel like teaching them."

"You what? That's crazy! You've finally got what you wanted, and now you don't want it anymore?"

She shrugged. "I think maybe I liked the *idea* of it more than actually doing it. It's like the fantasy of it was better than the reality."

He shook his head. "I think the sun's gotten to you."

Cathy sighed. "I don't know what's going on in this town, but I'm not sure I like it so much anymore," she said quietly. She paused to take a sip of champagne. "I've been thinking about how panicked I felt after getting all those responses, and how unexcited I feel now. I really thought this could be the Stream but…."

Bill cut her off before she could continue. "Relax, Cathy. Have some more champagne."

"No, Bill. I have to get this out coherently. I really think, now more than ever, that we have to remember the Stream, no matter how good we think things are here."

"But only time will tell if this really isn't the Stream!"

"But we know it's *not* the Stream! It's only the fourth town! How many times do I have to tell you this?" She realized her voice had risen, and she stopped hastily, looking around at the other patrons, but nobody seemed to be paying any attention.

"Cathy, think about it," Bill said. "In Plenty, all your needs are met. Right?"

She nodded.

He looked her in the eye, continuing. "You've met fascinating people who keep you engaged, as well as entertained. You are living in luxury and have enough free time to pursue everything you've dreamed of doing! You've got more art students than you know what to do with… I mean, you could start an entire art school if you wanted!"

"That may be so—and don't get me wrong, having all these desires fulfilled is great—but I don't want to confuse this with the Stream," she said quietly. "Think about it: if this was the Stream, don't you think I would be over the moon about having so many students to teach?"

Bill didn't seem to have an answer for her, and they sat in silence for a while.

"Okay, think about it like this," Bill finally said. "When you don't have what you want, you start to dream about it. Often the dream is better than the reality. It's only after we experience something in abundance that can we can know how much we really like it.

"When you didn't have any students, the thought of having them was totally exciting; but now that you have them, it's not the joy you thought it would be. Maybe this town shows us that when we have our needs and desires fulfilled in abundance, it frees us up to see what we really want. That's what's happening with you and the art students."

Cathy nodded, trying to process what Bill had said, and suddenly gasped. "Bill, that word: *Abundance*! This is without a doubt the town of *Abundance*!"

He smirked. "I think it should be the town of *Sex*."

Cathy rolled her eyes. "Bill, don't you think maybe your insatiable appetite for sex in this town is really a cover for your need to be loved and to connect with someone on a deeper level? Your need for sex is being met, but your need for intimacy isn't. How long do you think you can go on having meaningless relationships with countless women?"

His eyes twinkled, "I'm not sure… I'll let you know in a couple of years!"

Cathy frowned at him. "Bill, this isn't funny. You aren't going to be able to leave this town unless you let go of what you have here. I mean, I know you're having fun, but is this really what it's all about for you?"

Bill nodded.

At that moment, a young woman Cathy had never seen before came up to their table and whispered something to Bill. His eyes lit up.

"Sorry to bail, but I've got to dash!" he said, getting up and following the young woman out of the restaurant.

Cathy sighed. *I guess I'm on my own with this one*, she thought.

A few days went by before Cathy and Bill bumped into each other in the center of town.

"Bill, I really think we need to continue our conversation from the other day," Cathy told him.

He didn't look convinced. "I don't know what more there is to say," he replied.

"Come on, Bill, please. We have to address what's happening here!"

He sighed. "Fine, let's grab a drink."

As they settled in at a bar nearby, Cathy looked at him. "Bill, I've thought about this long and hard, and we've got to admit the truth: *Plenty* is not the Stream. It's great, but it's *not* the Stream. A lot of what I want is here, but it still feels like there's a vacuum inside of me. There's something that isn't being satisfied here."

"I can tell you how to get satisfied here," he smirked.

"Enough with the sexual innuendo!" Cathy felt like tearing her hair out. "Can't you see it's meaningless? All the sex in the world won't fill that void inside of you!"

"Look, Cathy: this town is it for me. I don't want anything more! Maybe this is *my* Stream."

"It doesn't work like that!" She was almost yelling, desperate to get through to him. "Can't you believe that everything you want will be at the Stream?"

"I can't imagine all these women being at the Stream…"

"But that's just it! You won't know until you get there, but you have to trust that what you *truly* want will be there!"

Bill went quiet, and his face became pale. "I never thought I'd be the one to say this, but… I think I'm stuck here. I can't move on from here yet."

Cathy nodded. "I totally get it. *Abundance* makes you think you have everything you could ever want. But, surely, too much of a good thing can be a bad thing as well."

Bill just stared at her. "Cathy, listen to me. I like it here, OK? I've got everything I want, and I don't think any of it is bad, so get off my case!"

"But Bill...."

"You can talk till you're blue in the face. I'm not budging from here! I've made my decision!"

Cathy felt her heart sink. "I've put too much energy on this journey fighting for others, and I'm not going to do it again," she said quietly. "I have to move on."

Bill seemed to soften at this. "But Cathy, how are you going to manage on your own?"

"I'll be fine," she assured him. "Maybe you'll change your mind and catch up to me!" she said, smiling.

Bill looked at her for a long moment, and she thought she saw a glimmer of realization in his eyes. But, instead of saying what she wanted to hear, he lifted his glass for a final toast.

The next morning, Bill met Cathy at the reception desk as she was checking out. It was one of the hardest goodbyes she'd had to say on her journey so far.

"I can't believe I'm actually going to do this alone," Cathy said quietly.

"There's still time to change your mind!" he said, hopefully.

"Likewise," she said, smiling. But she wasn't really holding out hope; she knew he didn't want to give up what he had here.

He walked her to the front doors, and hugged her tight as they said their goodbyes. "Good luck!" he whispered fiercely, and Cathy knew he meant it.

"Bye, Bill," she said softly. "I hope to see you again one day."

She kissed him on the cheek and walked out of the hotel, heading toward the beach. As she made her way along the turquoise ocean, the sounds of *Plenty* slowly began to fade behind her. She smiled to herself, happy in the knowledge that she'd been able to see beyond it.

CHAPTER 8

Contentment

Night had come so quickly that Cathy began to worry. The path had long since turned away from the beach, and the sound of the sea had faded. Everything was dark, except for the shining light of the full moon.

She took a deep breath and willed herself not to be afraid. She was all alone—that much was true—but she was *so* close to the Stream now. And with no one left to distract her now, she only had to keep going.

After walking for a couple of minutes, she saw twinkling lights on the horizon and rubbed her eyes in disbelief. Could this be the next town already? She started to run toward it, and within moments, she had arrived.

As Cathy entered the town, she found a guesthouse on the main street. It had a front garden and a white picket fence, and she could see through the large bay windows into a warm and comfortable living room.

She was embarrassed to be arriving so late, but she only had to knock once before a friendly, older lady answered the door.

"Welcome!" she said, giving Cathy a big smile.

"I'm so sorry to be arriving so late," Cathy said. "It's just that I didn't really know I would be coming here…."

"Don't worry, love. We're used to arrivals at all hours!" The woman laughed. "I'm Barbara, and you're most welcome here. You look like you need a nice cup of tea and a warm bath!"

Barbara let her in, and she booked a room for a few nights. As she was getting settled—the room was delightfully cozy and warm—Barbara knocked on her door, carrying a tray with tea and biscuits.

"Oh, thank you. That's so kind," Cathy said. She sincerely meant it, but she was so tired that she couldn't stop herself from yawning.

Barbara smiled. "You get a good night's rest, now," she said, setting down the tray. "You'll find yourself very busy here in *Contentment*!"

"*Contentment?*"

"Yes, dear, that's the name of this town."

Cathy felt a smile spread across her lips. "I like the sound of that!"

While she'd been walking, Cathy had been worrying that things wouldn't get any better than they had been in *Plenty*. But now that she'd arrived in the next town, she felt what could only be described as *home*. She drank her tea and had a few of the home-made biscuits, and then crawled into bed, feeling comfortable and safe, and drifted off into a peaceful sleep.

The next morning, Cathy awoke feeling well-rested and happy. She got dressed, whistling all the while, and went downstairs for breakfast.

As she entered the breakfast room, she couldn't believe what she saw.

"Richard!" she gasped. "What are you doing here?"

He beamed at her. "Cathy! It's good to see you!"

She ran towards him and gave him a big hug. This town was getting better and better.

"But I don't understand—how are you here? Why didn't we see you in *Plenty*? Did you even go to *Plenty*? How was *Faraway*? Did you find your money?"

"Whoa, one question at a time!" he said, laughing.

They sat down, and two cups of what smelled like freshly roasted coffee were put in front of them.

Cathy couldn't stop smiling. "I can't believe you're here!" she told Richard. "I was prepared to finish this journey on my own! I can't tell you how relieved I am to see you."

"Me too," he said sincerely, and then frowned. "What happened to Bill?"

Cathy rolled her eyes. "He got stuck in Plenty. There were too many…

distractions there. He couldn't see past it."

Richard nodded in understanding. "Yeah, that's an easy place to get stuck."

"So you've been there?"

"I had to. Everyone in *Contentment* has been through *Plenty*. You can't get here without going there first."

"How did you... No, wait. Tell me—what happened in Faraway? Did you find your money?"

He shook his head. "No. I searched for my business manager, but he was nowhere to be found. So I stuck around for a while, restarted my business and made all my money back."

She gasped. "Really? That's great! What happened after that?"

"Once I had my money back, I decided to move on. And, just like you said, I lost it all again when I got to *Loss*!" He shrugged. "I made a bad investment, and it was all gone again."

Cathy looked down at her coffee cup, remembering how important his money had been to him. "Richard, that's terrible," she said quietly.

He smiled faintly. "I thought so, too, at the time. I should've listened to you back then. You were right—no matter what I did, the same thing would happen when I got to *Loss*. The town makes you lose things that hold you back until you understand it and can move on."

Cathy shook her head. "I can't believe you had to go through all of that again!"

He fiddled with his spoon. "It was really tough, but I knew that if I stayed there to fight that battle all over again, I would never get to the Stream."

She looked at him. "So you understand now that everything you truly want will be at the Stream?"

"Yes. I do know that now. I realized that we have to understand each of these towns in order to move through them and not get stuck. I had to go back and go through that one again, so I could move on."

A thought occurred to Cathy. "Did you see Betty when you got to *Loss* the second time? We left her there, you know."

"Yes, I saw her. She told me you and Bill had moved on." He paused. "I spent a couple of days there, feeling devastated—depressed even—about my lost money. But I refused to wallow in my own sadness, and I left. Which is when I of course landed in *Plenty*."

"Isn't it beautiful there?" Cathy said, feeling nostalgic.

He smiled. "It is, but it's not without its limitations. I learnt quickly that once you experience an *abundance* of something, you no longer operate out of the fear of losing it. You're then able to release the fear. Once I understood this, I was able to make all my money back again!"

She laughed. "So after all that, you were still able to get your money back?" She sighed happily. "It's amazing how we've had such similar realizations, even though we've been on different journeys."

"On the contrary, Cathy. We're on the same journey!"

"True," she said, returning his smile. She sipped her coffee. "I wonder what this town is all about. I have to say, I like it here already!"

"Don't forget the Stream, Cathy…"

She rolled her eyes. "I'm not *forgetting* anything. But we have to figure out what this town is all about first, remember? I think I'm going to try and make my time here as constructive as possible."

He raised an eyebrow. "How are you going to do that?"

"I don't know, but I do know I plan to figure it out today!"

They finished their coffee and went their separate ways. As much as she was elated by her reunion with Richard, Cathy felt determined to make a success of her time in *Contentment* and knew that the way to do so would occur to her soon enough.

As she walked through the town, she spied a beautiful building with a 'to let' sign in the window. *That would make a wonderful art gallery*, she thought. She took a few more steps, and then she stopped and gasped.

"That's it!" she whispered. "I'll open my own art gallery!"

A few weeks later, Richard bumped into Cathy at the library. She was sitting at one of the tables, a stack of books in front of her.

"Richard, hi! Good to see you!" Her smile was genuine enough, but she sounded distracted.

"Hey, Cathy," he said, looking at the thick pad of notes she was scribbling. "What are you busy with?"

She sat back and looked at him, twirling her pencil. "Well, I've been thinking… What I did in *Plenty* was all wrong. I love art, but teaching was the wrong avenue for me. I've decided to open an art gallery, right here in *Contentment*!"

"That sounds great!" He looked at her bright smile and sparkling eyes, but found he couldn't quite feel happy for her—instead, he felt a sinking feeling in his stomach. "But… are you sure you want to do that here?" he asked gently.

Cathy was quiet for a moment. "Well, it's just that I feel I have to do *something* successful before I get to the Stream. And I think this is just the ticket!"

He nodded. "So how are the plans coming along? When are you going to open?"

"Well, there's just so much to do! I'm researching business models, and I've read all kinds of books on how to run a business. I'm drafting a business proposal as we speak."

"So you don't have a timeline?"

She stared at him. "I can't possibly have a timeline yet! There's too much I need to know before I can actually open the gallery."

He looked her in the eye and asked as kindly as he could manage, "Cathy, can't you see what's happening here?"

"What do you mean?"

"It's… Well, have you noticed that guy sitting over there?" He pointed to a man nearby, bent over his books, working furiously. Cathy shook her head. "Come with me," he said, beckoning.

Cathy got up and followed him. As they approached, the man looked up and smiled at Richard.

"Hi, Mark," Richard said. "This is my friend Cathy. Cathy, Mark."

"Pleased to meet you," he greeted her warmly.

"Mark is working towards his PhD," Richard explained. "He's done all his coursework; all he has to do is write his dissertation."

"Congratulations, Mark! That's wonderful!" Cathy exclaimed.

The man shrugged, "Yeah, it would be, if it wasn't for all this research! You can't be too prepared!"

"Mark's been researching for… how long was it again?" Richard asked him.

"Oh, about five years," he replied.

"Ah, that's right. Well, we won't keep you any longer," said Richard. "I know how busy you are. Good to see you."

As they got back to Cathy's desk, Cathy looked at him quizzically. "That's wonderful about Mark, but I don't understand. What's he got to do with my business idea?"

Richard sat down in the chair opposite hers. "Cathy, Mark has been researching his thesis for *five* years! He's got enough information to write *ten* theses—all he has to do is write it! Yet he hasn't started. And if you ask him why not, he'll give you a million reasons!"

She frowned. "Richard, getting a PhD isn't the easiest thing in the world, you know. I'm sure he wants to get it just right!"

"Well, I've spent some time getting to know him, and I think the truth is he's afraid."

Cathy stared at him, looking confused. "Afraid of what? That sounds crazy. He'll be able to do anything with a PhD!"

"Mark has spent his whole life trying to please his father," Richard explained. "His father always told him that he wasn't nearly smart enough to get a PhD, and the truth is he's afraid that his father might be right."

She tilted her head. "So, he's gotten this far, but he doesn't believe he can finish it?"

"Not exactly." Richard paused, trying to gather his thoughts. "It's more like… He's so caught up in the fear of failure that he's using his research as an excuse not to finish his thesis. This whole idea of being too prepared is a mask to hide the fear. If he writes the thesis but doesn't pass, he'll be crushed! That would confirm his father was right, maybe he isn't smart enough.

Cathy looked incredulous, "And you're saying this is all because his father put this idea into his head?"

Richard shrugged. "Something like that."

"I don't know about this," said Cathy, shaking her head. "I haven't had the easiest relationship with my mother, but that hasn't stopped me living my life!" she said, though her voice trembled slightly as she said it.

"Think about it," said Richard quietly. "People in *Contentment* have everything they need to achieve greatness—but then they just stop! It's like there's some invisible fence stopping them from taking the last step. Mark has been on the road to getting his PhD for years now, but he still doesn't have it just yet. His fear is actually *stopping* him from getting what he really wants."

Cathy was quiet for a moment. "So what are you trying to say?" she asked, her voice soft.

Richard took a breath. "I'm just saying that in this town, you could be researching your business proposal for years before you ever get around to opening your gallery."

"Richard, this is the way I have to do this! You can't just leap into things. I have to get everything right before I can move on!"

He held his hands up in defense. "I'm not saying that you should act on impulse, but in this town I think you should be wary of getting distracted and never actually following through and getting what you want."

She crossed her arms. "You may believe that, but I can't go ahead with this plan if I'm not prepared." Richard could see that he had touched a nerve, although she was trying to hide it. "And I'll never get anything done if you keep interrupting me," she continued cheekily.

"Fair enough. I'll let you get on with your work." He got up to leave, but turned back to her at the last second. "How about we meet next week on Saturday for dinner?" He wasn't prepared to leave her to her own devices in this town, even though he knew it was her business what she did.

"Sounds great," she said pleasantly, although her head was already back in her books.

The following week, Richard arrived at the guesthouse just as Cathy was walking down the stairs.

"Perfect timing," he said, winking at her.

Richard took her to one of his favorite restaurants in *Contentment*, a small, rustic Italian place with a beautiful courtyard in the back. They took a table outside, and he ordered them a bottle of Merlot.

"How's the business plan coming along?" he asked.

"It's going very well!" she replied—too quickly, he thought.

"Any concrete plans yet?"

She looked at him. "Richard, what's with all the questions?"

"Cathy, have you worked out for yourself what this town is all about yet?"

She shrugged. "Not exactly. But I know that it's comfortable and safe, and I'm very happy here!"

He looked down at his hands and took a deep breath. "I know we spoke about this at the library, but what I didn't tell you is that this is the town of *Integration*. Why do you think it's called *Contentment?* Not joy, not happiness. People here are merely *content* with what they have."

"So you think that because I like it here, it somehow means that I'm not integrated?"

"I think a clue might be to look at an area in your life where you're not moving powerfully in a unified direction, somewhere where you may be engaged in some distraction."

She seemed to consider this. "I guess that would be my professional life," she said slowly. "I've always wanted to do something involving art, but I've never been able to get it quite right. I'm hoping that this art gallery will solve that."

Richard was quiet for a moment. "Cathy, there's something I've been meaning to ask you. Remember at the library you said that you didn't always get along with your mother? What was that about?"

She smiled, although it wasn't a happy one. "I really don't want to talk about it."

But Richard didn't feel able to let it go—he wanted very much to keep her from getting stuck here. "You know you can trust me, right?"

"Yes, I know." She sighed. "It's just... she and I didn't always see eye to eye on things. She always used to push me to do what she wanted." She paused, seemingly miles away. "She often told me that I was useless, and I wouldn't amount to anything. Some kind of motivation!" She laughed, but her eyes were sad.

"Do you believe her?" he asked gently.

"Of course not!" Cathy sounded indignant. "I've got a degree; I've had plenty of jobs." She shrugged. "I refused to let her twisted mentality affect my life!"

"But don't you think, maybe, on some level, you *do* believe her? I mean, it was your *mother* saying these things, after all!"

"Richard, this is crazy." She looked at him, her eyebrow raised. "Are you trying to tell me that I'm useless?"

"Of course not!" He sighed. "Look, I really don't want to upset you, but if you can't see what's going on here, I'm going to have to tell you. No matter *what* you do in *Integration*, you won't achieve the greatness that you and I both know is inside of you. You think so little of yourself that you don't believe you can manage big things—being an art teacher, running an art gallery… they all feel too large for you. And as long as that's how you think of yourself, you won't be able to achieve great success."

She was shaking her head angrily. "Seriously, I don't know where you're getting this stuff." Cathy glared at him. "I've got big plans, and I will make them happen!"

"No, you won't," he said, as gently as he could manage. "Not as long as you're stuck here. You will make every excuse in the book not to open that gallery. You're afraid to confront the part of you that's holding you back—the part of you that you think is useless. And unless you do, you'll never get to the Stream!"

Cathy paled. "I've spent my whole life trying to prove that I'm not useless," she whispered. "Trying to show my mother that I *can* make something of myself… that I'm not a loser…."

He reached out and took her hand. "That's exactly why you're stuck. Instead of trying to prove it untrue, you have to confront it. If that means risking finding out that it's true, being useless—or being a loser—then so be it!"

She stared at him as if he'd slapped her. "Are you absolutely crazy? There's *no way* I'm ever going to say that I'm a loser! I'm not, and I *won't*!"

"Cathy, relax." He squeezed her hand. "It's okay. You need to start to see that this thought is now part of you. You think this way about yourself, and you need to embrace that truth. You need to stop trying to prove it wrong."

Cathy went quiet for a long time, staring at the tablecloth. "Do you really think I'm stuck here?" she whispered.

"Yes, I do," he said softly.

She shook her head. "I've just got to get something right before I move on. I really want to open this gallery, and I'm getting it together. I really am!"

"Cathy, are you hearing what I'm saying?"

"Yes, I am, and you're speaking nonsense!" Her anger began to flare up again.

"I promise you, Cathy, no matter what you do in *Contentment*, no matter how hard you try and fight it, you've got to confront this thing before you can move on and get to the Stream."

She stared at him in disbelief. "Richard, what's happened to you? Why are you saying these things?" She narrowed her eyes. "Did you bring some of Pedro's weed back from Faraway?"

"No." He laughed. "Just some things I've picked up along the way."

Cathy finished her wine. "I think I should get back. I've got a lot to do tomorrow, and I need to get some sleep!"

"I didn't mean to make you uncomfortable...."

"No, no, it's not that. I'm just really tired." She managed a small smile. "I'll see you around," she said.

As Cathy walked slowly back to the guesthouse, she felt troubled by what Richard had said.

By the time she got to her room, she was struggling to contain the emotion bubbling up inside her. All that talk about her mother had brought up feelings she'd thought long since squashed. She began to sob quietly. The scariest thing—the thing that made her feel the worst—was that she knew he was right. She was stuck.

Cathy woke up feeling exhausted. She hadn't slept well, and decided to call Richard so they could continue the conversation from the night before. He agreed to meet her for breakfast in half an hour.

When he arrived, Cathy was surprised to see that he was holding a bag.

"You're leaving?" she asked.

He nodded. "I have to go." He sat down and sighed. "But before I do, there's something I have to tell you. I wasn't completely honest before."

She blinked. "About what?"

"Well, the truth is, I've actually been to the next town. I just came back to fetch you."

She stared at him, shocked. "Really? I guess that explains why you knew what *Integration* was about all along! But…" she paused. "Why?"

Richard laughed, shaking his head. "I've had this thing my whole life about trying to rescue people. When I got to the final town, I met up with Seth. He told me that trying to help doesn't actually work, and the best thing for me was to keep going and get to the Stream myself." He shrugged. "I had to come back here in order to see it for myself."

She was flabbergasted. "I… I don't know what to say…."

He reached out and squeezed her hand, looking her in the eye. "The reason I pushed you like that about confronting the part of you that's holding you back is because *I* had to confront the part of me that wants to rescue people. Only now can I see that people are stuck where they are, and nothing I can do will change that. Trying to help is just a distraction. Now that I can see that, I can move on." He paused. "But I really hope that I'll see you again, when you're ready."

She looked down, fighting back tears. "I hope so, too," she said quietly. "But I just can't leave here. Not yet."

They were quiet for a long time before Richard got up. "Good luck, Cathy." He gave her a kiss on the cheek.

"Goodbye, Richard."

As he walked out the door, her heart sank. She was sad to see him go. She had believed for so long that she would make it to the Stream, but the thought of confronting a part of herself that she had buried down so deep for so long was too scary and painful for her just yet.

Richard made his way out of *Contentment* with a heavy heart. He knew that Cathy could only take the next step when she was ready.

The next part of the journey would be the toughest, and he knew it. He faltered for a moment, questioning his decision to leave *Contentment* again. He didn't know if he had the strength to face what would come next, but he realized that if he had done it once before, he could do it again. And what was on the other side was definitely worth it.

A strong wind pushed back against him, making him weave from side to side. He struggled to stay upright, and he began to feel sick, but willed himself to keep going. His body began to rock, and his stomach jumped into his throat. He began to tremble as his body went cold and numb.

Richard closed his eyes and thought of the Stream. It was the only thing that kept him going.

CHAPTER 9

Mastery

Richard opened his eyes. He couldn't quite remember when he had passed out, but he found himself on soft soil that felt warm and inviting. He gingerly sat up and looked around. He knew where he was—he'd been here once before, briefly—and he knew how to get to the final town: *Mastery*.

As the welcome sight of the town's outer reaches grew on the horizon, Richard reminded himself not to be seduced into the idea of settling in *Mastery*. It was the sixth and final town, but it wasn't the Stream. He had to find Seth, and although he had no idea where to look, he knew that he would find him, when he needed to. They would continue their conversation from last time.

As Richard walked toward the hotel he'd stayed in before, he marveled again at the town's architecture. Each building had been designed differently—you could tell each was unique to its builder.

There were beautiful parks on every corner, and a large lake lay at the edge of town. The climate was temperate, and everything grew and flourished here. He took a deep breath, and the clean air felt good in his lungs. Richard loved it here, and felt lighter and refreshed just being here, glad that he had decided to come back.

But not everything was perfect in *Mastery*. Richard noted the homelessness and poverty in the streets, creeping toward the designer boutiques and fancy restaurants frequented by the rich and powerful. *This town encapsulates life today*, he thought to himself. If he had a choice, he knew which side he wanted to be on!

Richard's revelry was interrupted by his arrival at the hotel, and the receptionist greeted him warmly. "Welcome back, Mr. Smith. Would you like the same room you had the last time?"

He smiled. "I would love that, thanks."

He climbed the stairs to his room, and immediately opened the curtains to gaze out of the floor-to-ceiling windows. The view was breathtaking: he could see as far as the horizon, and he stood there a while, marveling at what lay before him.

When the sun set, he decided to go down to the bar for a drink. The first person he laid eyes on was Seth.

"Seth! Am I glad to see you!"

Seth stood and clapped him on the shoulder. "Hey, Richard. Welcome back to *Mastery!*"

"Thanks. I missed this place!" he said with a smile.

Seth looked at him curiously. "How do you feel?"

"I feel... happy. Now that I'm here, I'm really eager to get the Stream."

Seth nodded, smiling. "One step at a time, Richard."

They walked outside and took a table on the terrace, sitting in silence for a while, just listening to the sounds of the waterfall nearby.

Seth broke the moment. "How is Cathy?"

Richard hesitated. "She's... where she is." He sighed. "I was really sad to have to leave her behind in *Contentment*, but I understand now that I can't rescue her. She has to take the last step of this journey on her own."

Seth nodded slowly. "It's difficult to do, especially when we care about someone, but I'm glad you realized that, and were able to come back here on your own."

"Me too." He paused. "To be honest, Seth, I'm pretty terrified about being back here. I don't know where to go, or what to do next."

Seth pushed his glasses up his nose but then lowered his chin to look over them. "Richard, the truth is that you've reached the place where you no longer *can* know. It's not about knowing here; it's the ultimate journey from here on out."

"Wait, so you mean I'm never going to know? But what am I supposed to *do*?"

Seth smiled faintly. "What you have to *do* is drop the idea of *doing* completely. In *Mastery*, it's not about knowing or doing. The only way you're going to get to the Stream is if you're taken there."

Richard frowned. "By who? Are you going to take me there?"

Seth held up his hands, signaling for him to slow down. "I know this is difficult to grasp, but what you need to do is *stop thinking*. Do you remember how in each town, you all thought so hard about how you were going to move on?"

"Yes, of course."

"Well, the problem all along was that the way you were thinking in those towns stemmed from the town *making* you think that way! Basically, your thinking could never have been part of the solution, and could never ultimately help you get out of those towns. The same applies to this town."

"So… are you proposing that I stop thinking?"

He laughed. "No, not to stop *thinking* altogether. But you will need to stop thinking about solutions to problems. What you need to do here is stop thinking about how you're going to solve the problem of getting to the Stream."

Richard felt like Seth was talking in circles. *Stop thinking about solving problems? How could you do that?*

Seth must have sensed his agitation, because he stood up and said, "I think I'm going to let you get settled and feel your way around *Mastery* for a while."

"Wait, Seth, don't go! Not yet!"

Seth looked at him and smiled. "You'll be just fine, Richard."

And with that, he was gone.

Richard spent his time in *Mastery* getting to know the town and its people. He made strong investments and watched his money grow, without feeling like he needed it or feeling attached to how much of it he had. He built a beautiful house with a huge garden, where he spent most of his free time swinging in a hammock. He made many new friends and socialized with like-minded people, where the conversation and laughter always flowed freely.

Eventually, he decided to get involved in politics, and after a few years, he ran for Mayor. He was elected, and the people loved him. He soon became the most powerful and respected member of the whole town.

He often found himself thinking about the Stream and wondering how it could be any better than what he had. Here, in *Mastery*, he had everything he had ever wanted, yet he *still* felt like something was missing. A part of him *knew* that there was still more than all of this.

One day, the doorbell rang unexpectedly. When Richard opened the door, he was glad to see that it was Seth.

"Hey! I'm glad you found me!" he said, beaming. "Please come inside."

"Hey, Richard. Beautiful house!" Seth said as he walked into the hallway, looking around.

"Thank you," Richard said, smiling. He felt proud of the paintings he'd collected, the ornate sculptures and ornaments that bedecked the tables, and the lush Persian carpets that covered the floor.

He led Seth into the den and poured them each a whiskey. Once they had settled, Seth came right to the point, "So how do you like *Mastery*?"

"I love it! It's better than my wildest dreams!" he exclaimed. "Everything I've ever wanted is here and within my reach. I feel so powerful ! And not just because I'm the Mayor of this town!"

Seth smiled fondly. "Yes, it's easy to get used to." He tilted his head. "Have you worked out what this town is all about yet?"

"I think so…" Richard hesitated, choosing his words carefully, "It feels like I'm so powerful here, and I make all the right choices… and things just seem to fall into place!"

Seth nodded. "Richard, this is the town of *Authority*. You take action here without blaming anyone, not even yourself, for the choices you make, or their consequences. You take the right actions, which give you perfect results." He pushed his glasses up his nose. "You keep moving on, even if you don't know where you're going, or what that result is going to be. You just know that you need to get there. You do not allow others to influence or hinder you. You are in a place of commitment, where you are moving forward powerfully."

"Yes!" Richard felt like Seth had summarized everything about his experience in *Mastery*. "But that sounds just like I imagined the Stream to be. So is this it?"

"Not exactly."

Richard frowned. "But I don't get it, then. Where *is* the Stream?"

Seth took a sip of his whiskey. "Richard, what do you think would happen if you let go of that feeling of power?"

He shook his head. "I have no idea. But I don't like the sound of that at all!"

Seth looked at him curiously. "Then, what if I told you that the only way to get to the Stream was by being buried alive?"

"What?!" Richard almost choked. "Are you crazy?"

Seth went on impassively, as if he hadn't said anything particularly strange. "Hypothetically, if that was your choice, would you die to get to the Stream?"

"I don't *want* to die! And I sure as hell don't want to be buried alive." Richard was incredulous. "After *everything* I've been through on this journey, after everything I've worked for, I'm supposed to give it all up and just die? By *choice?* You must be crazy!"

"I don't blame you for thinking so. But you still want to get to the Stream, right?"

Richard was quiet for a long time, twirling the ice cubes around in his glass. "I don't know anymore," he said softly. "I really like it here."

"Being here does *not* guarantee that you will never go back to *Either Way, Faraway, Loss, Plenty,* or *Contentment*. Look how easy it was to go back to Cathy. You might wake up one day and find yourself in *Loss,* and all of this will be gone. Are you prepared to risk that?"

"Jeez, Seth." Richard felt suddenly panicked. "I didn't realize that could happen."

Seth finished his whiskey and set the glass down. "Richard, this might be very tricky to grasp, but even in *Authority,* you are employing a strategy that is not aligned to your true intentions. The truth is you have to surrender your system— you have to surrender *everything.*"

Surrender? Richard thought. *Isn't that giving up?* Aloud he asked, "How do I do that?"

"On this journey of total surrender, you'll take the form of a seedling," Seth replied.

"A *what?*"

"A seedling. You will have to surrender your human form and become a seedling in order to be buried alive."

Richard shook his head, feeling like this conversation was way out of control. "I'm the Mayor of this town! You're crazy if you think I'm going to become some sort... some kind of... a *seedling,* and put myself in the ground intentionally!"

"Remember when we met, I told you about your Higher Self?" asked Seth, infuriatingly calm. "That Self knows how to get you where you want to go. But when you *try,* and when you employ a strategy, you can't get yourself to the Stream."

Richard felt like the world was starting to spin out of control. "But I think I am where I want to be! Aren't I?"

Seth shrugged. "You're asking the question, so I would say probably not. Is this," he asked, pointing to everything around him, "what you *really, truly* want?"

Richard sighed heavily. "Yes, you're right. I *want* to get to the Stream. I've come this far, and it's been in my sight for so long, I *have* to get there. So what do I do now?"

Seth's eyes twinkled. "Don't you remember what I said about *doing?*"

Richard rolled his eyes. "So, what? You're telling me I'm supposed to sit back and do *nothing?*"

Seth smiled. "This is where it gets interesting. You have to be in action—you have to be moving—and what that *really* means is holding an intention that is in alignment with the outcome you want. That intention will tell you what to do: you will start to receive urges and hunches, and by following those, you'll get there quicker."

"Whoa, whoa. Seth, this is getting way too complicated!"

"Just remember that all you need to do is hold the highest intention possible: being one with your Higher Self. And that, my friend, will take you to the Stream. By holding this intention and moving under its guidance, you will flow quickly to the Stream. It is only on this path and at the Stream that you will find eternal bliss." Seth looked at him, smiling gently. "So, Richard, are you prepared to do that? Are you ready to hold that intention?"

Richard was quiet. He found he had no idea *what* to say. Eventually he told Seth, "I just don't know *how*."

"Richard, there is *no* how. Remember that."

Seth bid him farewell, got up, and left. Richard stayed there, sitting alone in his den for a long time. He thought about what his life had been like up to this point. He thought about the people he had met, the things he had done, the places he had been. He thought about his journey, about the five other travelers who had gotten stuck on their way to the Stream. Eventually, he found he knew what he had to do.

He went upstairs and lay down on his bed. He closed his eyes and tried to relax and steady his breathing. He was so close now, he could feel it. He just had to *surrender*.

When Richard woke up, it was dark around him. He was somewhere moist and warm, and he didn't understand what was happening.

Then he remembered: he had completely surrendered!

His body ached, and he tried to move, but he was completely buried, under what felt like more soil than he could move. He felt himself being sucked further down.

Wait a moment. I don't want this! he thought. He started to fight and tried hard to claw his way out, kicking his legs and using all the strength he could muster to try to get out. Suddenly, he stopped. *This is what I want, isn't it?* He found he couldn't decide what he wanted to do. In the end, he decided to lie very still and calm his breathing.

He lay there in silence, closed his eyes and felt—nothing. Maybe he wasn't buried, exactly; he was in nothingness. Everything around him was dark. But he didn't feel scared or alone. He didn't feel cold, nor did he feel comfortable. He felt nothing.

After what seemed like ages, he took a large gasp and tried to fight his way out again. But again, he could change nothing. Richard began to sob; he felt that all was lost. He mourned the loss of his life, and he ached to be back in the warm sunshine.

Quite suddenly, he felt the most excruciating pain. It felt as if he were bursting at the seams. *Stop,* he tried to shout, but he wasn't making a sound. The pain continued; eventually, a root began to emerge out of him. It grew slowly, torturously, as it anchored itself in the soil beneath him. Quickly, another root sprouted, and suddenly he was surrounded by so many roots, he couldn't count them. He realized what was happening: *I'm growing!* he wanted to shout.

He began to rise up, and he soon reached the surface of the soil. He could see the sunlight through the cracks in the ground, and he could almost taste the sweet, fresh air above him. He was on the brink of becoming a tree, he realized, and happiness spread through him.

Finally, he surfaced, and he felt the sunlight warming up his body as he emerged from the soil.

As the sun shone down upon him, Richard slowly started to sprout leaves and branches, while he continued to grow towards the sky. He grew into a healthy, beautiful, vibrant tree. Over the years, Richard watched himself growing old and wise. Birds nested in his branches and different animals and insects began to depend on him.

As he grew, he came to realize his own power. He was one of the tallest trees in the area, and could cast shade onto the smaller trees whenever he wished: by his own strength, he could determine whether they lived or died. His trunk housed thousands of lives, and he knew that, on a whim, he could cast them out. He had never known power such as this in his entire existence.

He lived that power for hundreds of years. He felt like he was, literally, on top of the world. He dominated the other trees and lived in complete control. For ages, Richard stood there, high and magnificent in his beauty.

From time to time, Richard wondered about his traveling companions, especially Cathy: she'd come the closest. He hoped that they'd all eventually been able to conquer their fears, and that they, too, were experiencing the wonderful sense of power and destiny that he was feeling.

After many, many years, Richard's growth began to slow down. He was old, and his remaining time was running short. He had lived so happily as a tree, and he became afraid about what was going to happen next.

After everything he had been through, he couldn't understand why he would have to surrender again. But he knew in his heart that he had to.

He began to tremble as he felt complete *Ambivalence* over what to do next: Should he try to fight or should he surrender to his certain fate? He pondered and worried and wondered, but he couldn't decide what to do. Finally, he made a conscious decision to fight until he couldn't fight any longer.

He stood tall and firm, until he was over taken by a sense of nothingness. He found himself in *Alienation*, feeling disconnected from his roots and his surroundings.

He swayed in the breeze, feeling nothing, until a strong wind almost overpowered his trunk and destroyed many of his branches. He mourned the loss of his magnificence, as well as what he knew was his imminent death. He felt frightened and fearful as he found himself in *Abandonment*.

However, the sun continued to shine and the rain continued to nourish his roots and, before long, he had grown back most of his branches and leaves, even though they were only a fraction as beautiful as they had been. He basked in the experience of *Abundance*.

He knew what was coming next. After all, he had been there before. This time, though, when he found himself back in *Integration*, he knew that he was on the brink of his greatness: he was on the banks of the Stream.

And once Richard had returned to the greatest power he had ever known, *Authority*, he knew that he was ready to surrender once more.

Richard let go, completely and totally, and a large rumble could be felt all throughout the forest. His roots started to shrivel, and he began to lean to one side, ever further until with a mighty roar, he toppled to the ground.

The noise faded and the dust settled, and he lay there, slowly decaying and becoming one with the earth.

He began to feel something tickling him, and found he could hear the sound of moving water. It rushed over him, and he was overwhelmed by a sense of peace. All of a sudden he knew where he was: the Stream. He had surrendered, and was finally home, in the Stream.

Out of nowhere, he heard a whisper that seemed to come from all around him. "Welcome, Richard! I have been waiting for you. You are now a part of me. You are home!"

He was one with the Stream. He was at the source. It was like floating in heaven: the cool water rushed against him and surrounded him with love. He felt thankful for the utter peace and joy that he felt, feeling free and connected with his purpose.

Here, he was part of the Stream. Here, he would slowly fade away and all that he was would, in turn, feed the Stream. He had never imagined that he could connect with something as fully as this. This was it. This was true bliss.

Ultimate fulfillment.

Ultimate joy.

Ultimate peace.

Ultimate love.

www.ingramcontent.com/pod-product-compliance
Lightning Source LLC
Chambersburg PA
CBHW050502110426
42742CB00018B/3347